The SAS in Occupied France

The SAS in Occupied France

2SAS Operations
June–October 1944

Gavin Mortimer

Pen & Sword
MILITARY

First published in Great Britain in 2023
PEN & SWORD MILITARY
An imprint of Pen & Sword Books Ltd
Yorkshire – Philadelphia

ISBN 978-1-52676-958-9

Typeset by Concept, Huddersfield, West Yorkshire, HD4 5JL
Printed and bound in England by CPI Group (UK) Ltd, Croydon CR0 4YY

Printed on paper from a sustainable source by
CPI Group (UK) Ltd, Croydon, CR0 4YY

Pen & Sword Books Ltd incorporates the imprints of Aviation, Atlas, Family History, Fiction, Maritime, Military, Discovery, Politics, History, Archaeology, Select, Wharncliffe Local History, Wharncliffe True Crime, Military Classics, Wharncliffe Transport, Leo Cooper, The Praetorian Press, Remember When, White Owl, Seaforth Publishing and Frontline Publishing.

For a complete list of Pen & Sword titles please contact
PEN & SWORD BOOKS LTD
47 Church Street, Barnsley, South Yorkshire, S70 2AS, England
E-mail: enquiries@pen-and-sword.co.uk
Website: www.pen-and-sword.co.uk
or
PEN & SWORD BOOKS
1950 Lawrence Rd, Havertown, PA 19083, USA
E-mail: uspen-and-sword@casematepublishers.com
Website: www.penandswordbooks.com

Contents

This work is dedicated to

Sergeant Gerald Davis, and the men of Moussey,

who never talked.

How to use this book

This is a book for the committed battlefield tourist, and it might be an idea for those who can't speak a word of French to brush up on the basics! Unlike the majority of the First and Second World War sites, such as Thiepval, Arras and Normandy, the locations in this book are remote and rarely visited by battlefield tourists. That's hardly a surprise given that the SAS's task in the summer of 1944 was to conceal themselves in thick forests and deep ravines and to sally forth to wage guerrilla war on the Germans. In order to help you reach these sites, I've included the GPS coordinates in most cases. To pinpoint the exact location, on your computer open Google Maps and type in the coordinates that are shown as Decimal Degrees (DD): i.e., **47.82479, 2.484187**. A red pin will appear on your screen at the site.

Areas such as the Vosges and Bourgogne are stunning in their scenery and the people are warm in their welcome – but few speak much English, so be warned.

One other word of warning concerns hunters. You will be going into regions rich in game, and hunting is a massive pastime in France. The season begins in the middle of September and ends in February, and unfortunately French hunters have a well-deserved reputation for being trigger-happy. If you see a sign saying *'Attention! Chasse en cours'*, then a hunt is in progress so steer clear.

Another unwanted denizen of the forests in France are ticks but the forestry commission is diligent in posting signs alerting walkers to their presence – *'Attention aux tiques'*.

There are plenty of villages close to the sites mentioned in this book but they are sleepy, and what shops there are will be closed in the afternoons. Restaurants and cafés are few and far between outside the major towns but I have listed some of those where I found them. There are several good Second World War museums, which I have also listed, with some selling guide-books/pamphlets in English, as well as memorabilia connected to the war.

Talking of feet, bring sturdy walking shoes and a decent level of fitness. The SAS and the Maquis chose their camps well, and you'll only understand how well once you've trekked through the forest.

Happy hiking and remember, who dares gets the most out of this book.

Acknowledgements

Thank you firstly to those people in France who helped with the research for this book. In no particular order, Arnaud Blond, curator at the Museum of Resistance and Deportation in Lorris, the staff at the Museum of Resistance in Saint-Marcel, particularly Tristan Leroy and Christophe Guillouët, who kindly granted me permission to reproduce ten photos from the wonderful collection of Henri Costa. I am grateful also to Michel Diey and everyone at the 'Association des Amis du Châtillonais', Gerard Villemin, who was such a diligent and knowledgeable guide around the Vosges, as well as Maryvonne Arnoux-Bau, the former mayor of Le Mont, who not only showed me the location of the DZ onto which Henry Druce and his men landed, but also hosted me to lunch.

Sandy and Margot, my faithful 'support team', were as patient and tolerant as ever as we journeyed off the beaten track to pinpoint the events described in this book. Merci, mes belles!

Several villagers of Villaines-les-Prévôtes went out of their way to show me some of the exact locations of the action during the battle on that August evening, including the spot where Len Rudd lost his life. In Bierry-les-Belles-Fontaines I had the pleasure of meeting Maurice Rousselet, who shared his memories of life as a teenager in the village during the Occupation. Sadly, Maurice has since died, and also no longer with us is Henri Poirson. I had the privilege of meeting Henri in June 2016 and listening to his account of his time in the Maquis, including welcoming Henry Druce's advance party onto the DZ. Over a beer Henri spoke of his time in Auschwitz, rolling up one sleeve to show me his 92-year-old arm and the tattooed number still visible on his skin.

Jane Wadham, the daughter of Len Owens, whose courage, professionalism and sang-froid during Operation Loyton were so invaluable, provided me with much information about her remarkable father. Thank you, also, to Danielle Meier, for putting me in contact with Jane.

There are many corners of French fields in which there rests an SAS soldier. Most are remote and far removed from the large battlefield cemeteries of Normandy and the Somme. But thanks to the loving assiduity of such villages as Moussey, Moyenmoutier, Recey-sur-Ource and Villaines-les-Prévôtes the sacrifice of these brave young men endures.

Finally to the SAS veterans featured in this book, some of whom I interviewed and got to know well over the course of several years. Most are long since dead but their exploits endure. To Tony Greville-Bell, Arthur Thompson, Charlie Hackney, Bob Walker-Brown, Alex Robertson, Charlie Radford, Lew Fiddick, Harry Vickers, Bill Robinson and Henry Druce: 'You were men'.

Introduction

There have over the years been many inaccuracies and untruths written about the 2nd Special Air Service Regiment, some of them the fault of the regiment's founder, David Stirling. In fact the SAS was as much the brainchild of David's eldest brother Bill as it was his. During the war the joke among the soldiers was that SAS stood for 'Stirling and Stirling', and in his 1948 memoir, *Winged Dagger*, the superb 2SAS officer Roy Farran described the brothers as the pioneers of the 'SAS idea'.

In the semi-autobiographical *The Phantom Major*, published in 1958, David Stirling was quoted as saying he was captured in January 1943 in an attempt to drive north through Tunisia to become the first unit from the Eighth Army to link up with the First Army, of which Bill was a component, having 'recently arrived on the First Army Front with the 2nd SAS Regiment'.

In fact Bill was in Britain in January 1943 and 2SAS was not conceived until May that year. Bill did eventually arrive in North Africa in February 1943 as commanding officer of the Small Scale Raiding Force (SSRF). This was an amphibious unit that had been raised the previous year, ostensibly to attack Nazi targets in France, but in the winter of 1942/43 it was decided by Combined Operations HQ that the Mediterranean would be a more fertile hunting ground.

Bill Stirling's special forces' lineage stretched back further, to 1940, when he was one of six men selected to participate in Operation Knife, the purpose of which was to arm and train the Norwegian resistance in a guerrilla campaign against the German occupier. The six were members of an organisation called MI (R), a small clandestine outfit recently established by the War Office, and which was the forerunner of the Special Operations Executive (SOE).

The mission was aborted when their submarine hit a surface mine in the North Sea en route to Norway. Initially promised that a replacement submarine would be provided for a second attempt to infiltrate Norway, the six guerrillas were invited by Stirling to his country estate at Keir, just outside the town of Dunblane, where they were joined by Stirling's cousin, Simon Fraser, the 15th Lord Lovat. It was here that Stirling conceived the idea of a guerrilla training school. 'It was thanks to Stirling's imagination and initiative that our partnership was not, in fact, immediately dissolved,' said Tony Kemp, one of the six.

David Stirling.

The 6ft 5in Stirling was a wealthy landowner, a man of influence, and he persuaded the War Office to agree to the establishment of the training centre. It helped that, as he pitched the idea, Neville Chamberlain was replaced as Prime Minister by Winston Churchill, a man who approved of irregular warfare.

'It was Stirling's idea that the six of us, reinforced by a few selected officers and NCOs, should form the nucleus of a new training school,' said Kemp. 'We should begin with cadre courses for junior officers from different units of the army.'

The training school was located in the north-west of Scotland, close to the sea, the moors and the mountains. It was officially designated the Commando STC (Special Training Centre) and for nearly a year hundreds of officers graduated after a two week course in fieldcraft, unarmed combat, kayaking, demolitions and small arms instruction, among them David Stirling.

Bill Stirling subsequently went to Egypt with the SOE before becoming the private secretary to General Arthur Smith, the chief of the general staff at Middle East HQ in Cairo. It was in the Egyptian capital that Bill and David, who was part of the Layforce commando outfit, produced a memorandum proposing a small airborne commando unit to attack enemy targets in Libya: the SAS.

The Stirling brothers.

Three members of 2SAS pose for the camera while training in Scotland in the spring of 1944.

Bill was recalled to Britain in early November 1941, just days before the disastrous inaugural raid by the SAS, and after a disagreement with the War Office he left the military and returned to his estate in Scotland. It was an appalling act of mismanagement on the part of the War Office, the inexcusable squandering of a brilliantly unorthodox military mind. Eventually, someone in the War Office came to their senses and in October 1942 Bill Stirling was appointed commanding officer of the SSRF.

The harsh winter of 1942/43 rendered amphibious operations in the Channel impractical and, together with the rapidly changing situation in North Africa, Bill Stirling saw an opportunity to transfer the SSRF's area of operations. He brought his force to Philippeville, now Skikda, on the Algerian coast, and on 13 May 1943 the SSRF was reconstituted as 2SAS with a strength of 450 men. Roy Farran was one of the first recruits. He described Bill Stirling as 'a mountainous man, who shook us warmly by the hand and asked us a few embarrassing questions. He radiated an encouraging aura of confidence.'

The formation of 2SAS was the easy part; harder was to convince 15th Army Group of how the regiment should be deployed in the impending invasion of Sicily and Italy: strategically and not tactically. The disagreement foreshadowed events of the following spring.

After operations in Italy, 2SAS returned to Britain in late March 1944 and became part of the 2,500-strong SAS Brigade under Brigadier Roderick William McLeod, a veteran army officer but without any experience of special forces. He answered to Lieutenant General Frederick 'Boy' Browning, commander of the 1 Airborne Corps, which was part of 21 Army Group.

On 4 April 1944, 21 Army Group issued an operational order that stated the role of the SAS Brigade in the invasion of France would be 'attacks on suitable types of objectives in the concentration areas of hostile mobile strategic reserves behind the length of the French Channel coast'. In essence, the SAS was being told to parachute into 'an area inland from the coast to a depth of 40 miles' as and when German Panzer reserves were observed moving towards the beachhead. Lightly armed, the SAS men's only advantage would be if they had the element of surprise on their side, but the chances of parachuting into enemy territory without being seen were very slim.

Once again Bill Stirling had to argue the SAS case with senior officers who did not grasp their *raison d'etre*. One 2SAS officer, Major Sandy Scratchley, described the dispute 'as a hell of a rumpus'. Although he was supportive of Stirling's stance, Scratchley accused his CO of some 'tactless criticism'. Brigadier McLeod bore the brunt of Stirling's wrath and when he refused to make an official complaint to 21 Army Group about their orders, Stirling protested to Lieutenant General Browning. 'Browning sided with Stirling, so McLeod had to appeal over Browning's head to [Field Marshal] Montgomery, who sided with him,' recalled M.D.R. Foot, a staff officer in the SAS Brigade.

Field Marshal Montgomery, seen here addressing the SAS in 1943 prior to the invasion of Sicily, had a hand in Bill Stirling's dismissal as CO of 2SAS.

'Stirling went to Eisenhower, who took the opposite view. McLeod had to go to Downing Street and get Churchill to resolve the problem in his favour. Stirling went back to Keir in plain clothes.'

The news of Stirling's dismissal was a shock for the men under his command. Approachable, intelligent and empathetic, Stirling was respected and admired by 2SAS, all of whom shared his anger at their initial orders.

'It was ridiculous, we were to be dropped within 15 miles of the front, one place you don't want to be,' reflected Major Tony Greville-Bell. 'We were absolutely in agreement with Bill and in fact the senior officers, of whom I was one then, were inclined to resign . . . but Bill told us not to. And we were lucky to get Brian Franks, who was a brilliant officer.'

Franks had been the brigade major of the Special Service Brigade and had seen the SAS at close hand during the bloody battle of Termoli in Italy in October 1943. He had been awarded a Military Cross for his action over several days of fighting, the citation praising his 'fine sense of initiative and complete disregard of personal danger' when the battle was at its fiercest and a German counter-attack was on the brink of retaking the Italian port.

Major Sandy Scratchley (*left*) and Roy Farran at Termoli.

Stirling had sacrificed his career for the SAS Brigade, but it was not in vain. Shaken by the furore, 21 Army Group re-examined the planned tactical deployment of the SAS and concluded that Stirling had been correct in his analysis. Furthermore, it had dawned on 21 Army Group that the airborne divisions would require all available aircraft on D-Day and for the following 48 hours, and therefore there would be no means of delivering the SAS to their drop zones.

Instead, the SAS would be used in a strategic role, dropped hundreds of miles inside Occupied France to arm and train Resistance groups, and also to act as an intelligence link to the SOE agents already operating in the areas. 'In general, SAS operations were now planned to take place from 50 to 400 miles in advance of the main Allied armies,' wrote Colonel Terence Otway in the official history of the Airborne Forces.

Drawing on the advice of the Resistance (or Maquis) and the SOE agents, the SAS would establish bases in the area of operations where they could organise offensive operations and the resupply of arms, equipment and men. Small advance teams would parachute into the area ahead of the main SAS party, accompanied by liaison personnel from Special Forces Headquarters codenamed 'Jedburghs', usually a three-man team comprising a British officer, a French officer and a British or French wireless operator. Their role was to establish contact with the local Maquis groups, a task that often required a touch of diplomacy as there could be political factions at play among the various bands.

By the start of June the SAS Brigade knew they would be deployed strategically in France but the precise nature of their operations was dependent on the main operational plan, i.e. the Normandy invasion. As Otway explained in the official history of the Airborne Forces, the factors that remained unknown until the last minute in all SAS operations in France were:

(a) The size of the party.
(b) The distance of the operational areas from the main battle.
(c) The probable duration of the operations.
(d) The type of initial equipment required.
(e) The action by personnel after operations – i.e. whether they would remain where they were and be maintained by air, or whether they would make their own way through our lines.
(f) The intentions and preparations of other organizations involved, such as the S.O.E.

2SAS were to suffer more than 1SAS in the planning of operations in France. Regarded as more callow than their sister regiment, 2SAS were held in reserve throughout June as all four squadrons of 1SAS were inserted into France. Indeed, throughout this month 2SAS were still 100 men shy of the intended fighting strength of 425 and that meant recruiting men without thorough physical and psychological screening. This was to have ramifications when they did eventually insert into enemy territory.

2SAS operations got under way in July and while Wallace-Hardy was a success, others, notably Loyton, were not. This, concluded a brigade report written in December 1944, was because 'they were developed too late ... the very swift advance of Allied armies was mainly responsible, together with the difficulties of mounting the air operations at an earlier date owing to the short hours of darkness'. The report then listed 2SAS casualties:

- Lost in Aircraft   8
- Killed   16
- Believed POW   14
- Missing   40

Those listed as missing were in fact dead, tortured and executed by the Nazis who were obeying Adolf Hitler's 'Commando Order' of 1942. The first the regiment knew of the Order was when Lieutenant Jimmy Hughes reached Britain in May 1944, four months after he was badly wounded during a 2SAS raid on an Italian airfield. But for the extent of Hughes's injury, he would have been shot in the days after his capture, but he was helped to escape by a sympathetic German doctor who was morally opposed to the Commando Order. After an epic trek through Occupied Italy, Hughes finally reached the Allied lines and was flown back to the UK. The SAS compiled a detailed report based on his testimony but in what became known as the 'Hughes Case' the report was dismissed by 21 Army Group as 'a mere German interrogation technique'.

Jimmy Hughes.

Dozens of 2SAS soldiers were murdered by the Nazis in France, including Hughes's former sergeant, Ralph Hay, with whom he had served in Italy. After the war 2SAS vowed to track down the killers and bring them to justice for, as one of the executed said in the moments before his death, 'We were good men'.

Chapter One

Operation Trueform

The first 2SAS operations launched in Occupied France were not fruitful. Ineffectual and innocuous, they achieved little and the only saving grace was that the regiment did not sustain heavy casualties. This was not the fault of the men who participated in Operations Defoe, Dunhill, Rupert and Trueform; rather the blame lies in part with 21 Army Group, which inserted the parties too late in the summer for them to make an impact, but also the fact that 2SAS arrived in the UK from Italy on 17 March and were still in the process of recruiting and training when the Allies invaded France on 6 June militated against their chances of success. 1SAS, on the other hand, had been in the UK since the start of January 1944 and it was only natural that to them fell the honour of embarking on the SAS Brigade's first operations in France, along with the two French regiments.

2SAS's turn came finally on 19 July, the day after General Bernard Montgomery, in command of Allied ground forces in Normandy, had launched Operation Goodwood, the purpose of which was to expand the bridgehead established by the Airborne Brigade on 6 June. The offensive commenced in the early hours of 18 July with a terrifying aerial bombardment delivered by 2,000 Allied bombers. 'It was a bomb carpet ... the most terrifying hours of our lives,' recalled Werner Kortenhaus of the 22nd Panzer Regiment. 'Among the thunder of the explosions we could hear the wounded scream and the insane howling of men who had been driven mad.'

The armour and the infantry came after the aerial assault and, as they thrust against the German defences, several miles to the south, in the Argentan region of southern Normandy, twenty-two soldiers from 2SAS commenced Operation Defoe. The two officers in charge were interesting characters.

Lieutenant James Silly was only 20, the son of a distinguished father who, as an airman in the First World War, had been awarded a Military Cross and a Distinguished Flying Cross. Not long after joining the SAS in the spring of 1944, Lieutenant Silly, who preferred to be called 'Jim', learned that his father, now an air commodore, had died in a Japanese POW camp in Hong Kong.

Twenty-five-year-old Captain Bridges George MacGibbon-Lewis (often frequently misspelt as McGibbon) had been commissioned into the Black Watch in 1940 and the following year he fought in the battle of Crete. He fled the island in an abandoned landing craft, only for his enterprise to be foiled by an

Italian submarine. He escaped from his POW camp in September 1943 after Italy's surrender and, in the company of a fellow officer, traversed 250 miles by foot, train and boat to reach Allied lines. MacGibbon-Lewis subsequently volunteered for 'A' Force, a deception unit established by Brigadier Dudley Clarke, one of whose responsibilities was to rescue some of the thousands of former Allied POWs who had been released from their camps following the Italian surrender. MacGibbon-Lewis was awarded a Military Cross for his work in leading scores of POWs to safety, the citation praising his 'courage and determination'.*

The operational instructions issued to MacGibbon-Lewis and Silly were to conduct a reconnaissance in depth, radioing back intelligence on enemy troop dispositions and calling up RAF air strikes if necessary.

Operation Defoe quickly became subsumed by greater events. Although Operation Goodwood had not achieved the results as swiftly as Montgomery had hoped, the Germans' dogged resistance had cost them greatly in terms of men and machines lost: 109 tanks destroyed, half their complement of anti-tank guns gone and hundreds of soldiers killed or captured. On 22 July the German commander-in-chief, Günther von Kluge, wrote to Hitler warning that 'the moment is fast approaching when this overtaxed front line is bound to break, and when the enemy once reaches the open country a properly co-ordinated command will be almost impossible'.

Three days after Kluge's letter, the Allies launched another offensive, this time on the western side of the bridgehead. Like Goodwood, Operation Cobra was preceded by a huge aerial bombardment in the St Lô area and then three infantry divisions of General Omar Bradley's First Army advanced. Once again, the Germans fought valiantly, the Americans progressing just 2 miles on the first day of Cobra. But their reserves of courage had been drained and, unable to continue resisting the 120,000 troops ranged against them on a 5-mile front, the German line broke. By 28 July the hole punched by the Americans was 15 miles deep. To turn the breakthrough into a breakout, Bradley called on Lieutenant General George S. Patton.

Defeat for Germany in France was inevitable. On 8 August the Canadians launched Operation Totalise, the first act in the closing of the Falaise pocket. It required two more weeks of intense fighting before Canadian and Polish forces linked with American troops advancing from the west.

The German Army Group B was spent. Some 200,000 were prisoners and a further 50,000 had been killed in the ten weeks since D-Day. Two of the eleven Panzer divisions – Lehr and the 9th – had lost all their tanks. There was nothing for the survivors to do but withdraw east towards Germany, chased by Patton's Third Army.

* MacGibbon-Lewis enjoyed a successful post-war career as a record producer, composer and music manager, and one of his songs was featured in the Cliff Richard film 'Express Bongo'.

The collapse of German resistance in Normandy had repercussions for 2SAS. Operation Defoe became largely irrelevant. Men went out on reconnaissance patrols but there was nothing to reconnoitre. One soldier, 24-year-old Private James Wilkinson from Liverpool, was killed by a booby trap on 5 August. Ten days later MacGibbon-Lewis did lead one small reconnoitre for the 2nd Army to gather information on German positions in the triangle created by the towns of Falaise, Argentan and Flers.

Eventually, on 23 August, two days before the liberation of Paris, Brigadier Maurice Chilton of the 2nd Army HQ, gave MacGibbon-Lewis a letter to pass on to Roderick McLeod, brigadier of the SAS Brigade, on his return home. 'The Det[achment] of 2SAS Regt. which was attached to us is returning to England to rejoin its Regt,' he wrote. 'I think it has been proved that conditions are not really favourable for their employment close in behind the enemy lines. The battle is either too static or too fluid for the type of task we had in mind and by waiting for perfect conditions it meant retaining your very valuable officers and men for long periods doing nothing, which is obviously unwise when there must be so many suitable tasks for them on a bigger scale.' Nonetheless, Chilton lavished warm praise on 2SAS, stating that everyone in the 2nd Army 'was most impressed by the enthusiasm and good spirit and type of work done by the detachment'.

Unfortunately, what was true of Operation Defoe was applicable to several other 2SAS operations launched in August. On the third night of that month Captain Tony Greville-Bell led fifty-nine men into France in an area between Rennes and Laval. 'I didn't know what the operation was called,' reminisced Greville-Bell, who had been awarded a DSO in Italy the previous year for a successful sabotage mission. 'But I know it was a complete waste of bloody time.' In fact the operation was codenamed Dunhill, but within hours of parachuting into Allied-held territory, Greville-Bell and his men encountered the advance elements of the American Third Army.

Simultaneous with Dunhill was Operation Rupert, launched on 4/5 August under the command of Lieutenant Douglas Laws with instructions to sabotage the railway lines in eastern France between Nancy and Chalons-sur-Marne. In fact the operation had been scheduled for the previous month but the Stirling bomber carrying the advance party had crashed into a hillside as it approached the DZ on the night of 23 July. Among the dead were the party's leader Major Felix Symes and Private Len Curtis, both veterans of operations in Italy the previous year.

It was a further fortnight before the replacement advance party was dropped (a delay caused by the moon periods) and on 12 August two further sticks led by Lieutenants Cameron and Marsh were inserted. Cameron was nicknamed 'Loopy', an affectionate name bestowed by his men who attributed his sometimes eccentric behaviour to a head wound sustained earlier in the war. He wrote after the war that the situation in France was 'confused'. He continued: 'The Germans knew they had had it and their morale was falling daily ... we followed in their wake, the way littered with their wrecked and smoking transport, never knowing what the next corner would bring.'

By the second half of August the SAS had been overtaken by the American Third Army. For a short period the Americans encouraged the SAS to act as their eyes and ears, but then General Patton arrived. 'We hoped to move east and link up with those 2SAS boys on Operation Loyton [see Chapter 4],' recalled Cyril Radford, one of the soldiers on Rupert. 'But when Patton came along he put a stop to that. He didn't like the British so he gave orders for us to be escorted out of the Third Army area by US MPs [military policemen].'

The forty men from 2SAS who parachuted into Normandy as part of Operation Trueform on 16 and 17 August were in the rear of the American advance, but they nevertheless encountered many Germans, withdrawing in a disciplined fashion from Brittany. Trueform was launched in the rolling countryside south of Rouen and north of Evreux. Their tasks were to destroy German petrol supplies for their retreating motor transport, 'general harassing of the enemy' and radioing back information on the military situation.

Four parties were inserted into the operational area, but we shall concentrate on just one, which suffered the two fatalities of Operation Trueform. Party No. 1, commanded by Captain Richard Holland, parachuted on the night of 16/17 August. Holland, a vicar's son, was a pre-war regular, the

'Loopy' Cameron, Bill Robinson (*at the wheel*) and Cyril Radford (*in the rear*) prepare to embark on a patrol during Operation Rupert.

Charlie Radford (*third from left, partly obscured*) in Italy in 1945, a few months after he took part in Operation Rupert.

Captain Richard Holland (*back row, far left*), and some of his men on Trueform find something to laugh about.

recipient in May 1940 of a Military Cross for his valour during the battle for Calais, although he was inexperienced as an SAS operative.

Holland and his ten men parachuted onto the correct DZ, on farmland just south of the village of Bonneville-Aptot, just after midnight on 17 August. Holland split his men into three sticks of four, four and three. One party under Colour Sergeant Major William Ellis moved west, that commanded by Lance Corporal Conroy headed south and Holland set off to the north. At 0730 hours Holland and one of his men, Bosson, approached a farmer. 'He was very suspicious,' wrote Holland in his report. 'After 30 minutes' persuasion he fetched the son of the village leader of the French Resistance, called Alfonse.' Alfonse Marais had thoughtfully brought some food for the soldiers and his father, and after their nourishment, the SAS discussed with the Resistance the possibility of an ambush. They decided on a suitable location on the road, and agreed the attack would take place the following evening. 'But they called it off at the last moment on account of orders from above that no action was allowed until the Allies were within 25 kms distance,' remarked Holland.

In scouting an ambush site, Holland encountered three of his men, William Cooke and Searle and Sapper Harry Erlis, an ex-Royal Engineer, who had become separated from CSM Ellis as they fled from a German patrol.

On the morning of 19 August Holland and his men reconnoitred south, past the village of St Éloi-de-Fourques, emerging from a wood to look down on the hamlet of Le Buhot. On the north-east outskirts of the hamlet was a

Members of the Maquis gather for a ceremony in the forest close to St Éloi-de-Fourques.

farm owned by a man called Bardel, and Holland 'discovered possibilities of destroying German vehicles in the farm yard'. The Maquis cautioned against such a strike, explaining that the reprisals of the Germans would be brutal. Instead it was agreed to lay some tyre busters on the road that ran past the farm towards the town of Brionne to the west.

Holland ordered three of his men, Sapper Erlis, Private John Burke and Private Thomas Bintley, a married man from Liverpool who had volunteered for the Parachute Regiment from the King's Shropshire Light Infantry in January 1944, to carry out the act of sabotage. They were accompanied by Alfonse Marais of the Resistance. There are conflicting reports about the subsequent chain of events. According to Holland's report, the quartet were 'tempted off to the farm' with the aim of placing some incendiary bombs among the German vehicles. 'When they were creeping up on the transport they came upon four Germans who promptly gave themselves up,' wrote Holland. 'While these were being taken care of, sixteen more SS, including an officer, surrendered. At that moment, however, some Germans from the road started shooting and there was considerable confusion.'

Holland's account seems improbable. The SS were not in the habit of surrendering, particularly at this stage of the war, and certainly not to inferior numbers of enemy. The version provided by Monsieur Bardel, who owned the farm at Le Buhot, seems to be more plausible. Describing how a detachment of SS – he estimated their strength to be 150 – arrived at his farm, Bardel continued: 'One of them entered the wood and met a group of three or four English parachutists who, being with the Resistance of St Éloi-de-Fourques, used to come to me in search of food. In a few moments a fight began. There was fire and counter fire. One of the parachutists was killed, another taken prisoner.'

The dead man was Bintley, killed by a bullet to his head. He and Erlis were pals, a couple of lads from Liverpool, and Erlis was captured as he tended to his dying friend. Also caught was Alfonse Marais. John Burke accounted for at least one German, and then escaped through the woods to make his report to Captain Holland. (Burke was awarded a Military Medal in 1945 while serving under Roy Farran in Italy, for his part in a daring attack on a Nazi HQ. The citation commended his 'remarkable courage . . . his intelligence and initiative'.

'The Germans beat us,' recounted farmer Bardel. 'Then they forced Marais and me to dig a grave for Bintley. They made us dig it in a refuse pit. While we performed this duty they danced on the corpse of Bintley.'

Erlis, recalled Bardel, was forced to empty his pockets. His money and cigarettes were divided among the Nazis. He was asked where the rest of his comrades were. Erlis declined to answer. He was repeatedly beaten and then asked the same question. Each time he said nothing, and each time he was struck again with a little more force. The last sighting of Erlis was four days later, not far from the farm, where he was 'very carefully guarded'. Two months later his body was washed up on the banks of the river Seine. He had no boots and his hands were bound behind his back, but the body was too decomposed 'to see if there had been any violence'.

Holland said that the fateful contact 'upset the French' and they called off a joint attack they had planned for that evening. Holland and some SAS soldiers attempted at nightfall to throw some Lewes bombs in German trucks as they drove along the road 'but they were going too fast'. A Lewes bomb, named after its inventor Jock Lewes, one of the original SAS officers, was composed of plastic explosive and thermite, rolled in motor car oil, and fitted with a detonator, instantaneous fuse and a time pencil. It was held in a linen bag, about the size of a glove, and was light enough to throw but powerful enough to destroy a vehicle or aircraft.

The next night the SAS observed several Tiger tanks trundling down the road to Evreux and the following evening, 21 August, Holland and his men ambushed a convoy just north of the village St Éloi-de-Fourques on the road that linked Brionne to Rouen. A tyre-buster took out the wheels of the truck at the head of the convoy, and the soldiers raked the cab with machine-gun fire. 'This caused considerable confusion and shouting, and we heard the noise of motor-cycles rushing up and down the convoy,' recorded Holland.

(*Left to right*) Maquis chief André Couturier, 2SAS officers Lieutenant Boris Samarine and Captain Holland, and Abbe Sanquer, the priest of St Éloi-de-Fourques.

The next day it rained, and it didn't stop for the next 24 hours. The French abandoned an attack, to Holland's chagrin. 'There was no cover from the rain but that was no excuse,' he reflected. 'My men were also browned off and unwilling. It was disappointing as the roads were full of German traffic.' Spirits lifted when the rain did, and on 23 August the SAS 'blew up a truck and shot at some marching infantry'.

Meanwhile Lance Corporal Conroy, who had headed south from the DZ with Privates Walsh and Keane, had experienced some adventures of his own. They had seen the SS column arrive at the farm at Le Buhot from their hideout in the woods to the north, and had trekked east for a mile or so. Then they turned south-west, scouting the road between Brionne and Harcourt, encountering a local youth as they did so. Once he had overcome his initial fright, the boy disappeared but soon returned with some bread and cider. His father accompanied his son and guided the three soldiers to the quarry where he worked, and showed them a tank of fresh water. By the evening of 18 August Conroy had been introduced to a Maquis group, and they in turn brought to the British a member of the Special Operations Executive who was operating in the area. Briefed by Conroy on their intention to carry out sabotage attacks on the Germans, the SOE agent said it was a 'hopeless' task. During this nocturnal discussion, 'Germans were heard talking about 50 yards away'. One of the Maquis understood the language and 'explained to us that the Germans were aware of our presence in the wood'.

On the morning of 21 August the SAS slipped out of the wood just as the Germans began an encirclement. The area was teeming with Nazis and Conroy reached the same conclusion as Holland had done, just a few miles away: namely, that they were in a most unhealthy predicament. Fortunately the cavalry arrived in the form of the 2nd Canadian Division, which had advanced south following the surrender of the German Seventh Army in the Falaise Pocket, the offensive that marked the end of the battle of Normandy.

The Canadians were surprised to encounter a detachment of British soldiers so far south and Holland noted that 'we were nearly shot at by an armoured column'. Once credentials had been established, there were warm handshakes and, on 25 August, a 'victory march followed by more cere-monies at War Memorials'. The next day a memorial service was held at the church of St Éloi-de-Fourques for Thomas Bintley, which 'was attended by the French Resistance in force, and all the village'. Afterwards Holland and his men left for 1 Canadian Corps HQ and thence to England. He departed with the gratitude of the French, who handed him a letter on August 26:

From the day that the Germans have withdrawn from French territory because of the effort of our allies, the FFI of our Maquis have wanted to express their profound affinity and their gratitude for the great effort that you have made for the liberation of our country. We would like you to pass on these feelings of gratitude to your men and also your army, that this friendship created in the name of freedom will be the guarantee of our alliance.

Lance Corporal Conroy and his section followed a couple of days later, along with CSM Ellis, who had staggered into Brionne on 17 August 'in a badly exhausted condition'. Ellis had been posted on attachment to the SAS in November 1943 from the Royal Army Physical Training Corps, and he had required all his mental and physical stamina during the previous week. Separated from his party within hours of parachuting into France, Ellis had nonetheless attempted to harass the enemy whenever possible. On the evening of 23 August he had used pocket incendiaries to destroy two staff cars west of Bonneville-Aptot, and the following evening, close to the same spot, he shot dead two Nazis. He had subsisted on apples and turnips and tried without success to contact the Resistance. His ordeal ended on 25 August when he met a Canadian reconnaissance party a mile to the east of the village of Villez-sur-le-Neubourg, and 8 miles east of Brionne.

In total Operation Trueform (which also included a detachment of Belgian SAS troops) killed five Germans – in reality, the number was significantly higher but as most attacks occurred at night the exact figure could not be ascertained – and captured seventy-eight. At least twenty-five trucks were destroyed or immobilised, two convoys ambushed and five dumps – three ammunition, one food and one petrol – were blown up. It was a very modest tally considering the number of men who had participated in the mission. They had lacked nothing for courage but, as Holland noted in the conclusion of his report, it is 'a severe handicap if troops have no previous battle experience'. Ultimately, however, Operation Trueform suffered from inadequate planning, which was the responsibility of 21 Army Group. 'The country in which they were dropped was not very suitable for SAS operations or for overt resistance,' concluded an SAS Brigade report into 2SAS operations. 'And it is open to question whether, if given more time, they would have been able to prove themselves worthwhile. Most of their reports complain that the short duration of their operations rendered them virtually useless, but this was one result of the speed of the Allies' advance after the Seine had been crossed.'

What to visit

St Éloi-de-Fourques

There are few sites to visit when retracing the steps of Operation Trueform because of the brevity of the mission and the fact the men were constantly on the move to avoid the Germans as they passed through on their way to the Fatherland. The countryside, as the post-operation report commented, was not suitable for guerrilla operations, but it is for cycling, with few steep hills

St Eloi-de-Fourques.

but plenty of agreeable scenery. Touring the region on a bicycle is an ideal way of getting around.

The drop zone of Captain Holland and his men can be found on farmland to the south of the village of Bonneville-Aptot (**GPS 49.254195, 0.764695**). From there head south on the D92 to St Éloi-de-Fourques. The village church (**GPS 49.231948, 0.794800**) was where Holland and his men, along with villagers, attended a memorial service to Thomas Bintley on 26 August. Outside the church is the village war memorial.

Le Buhot

Head south from St Éloi-de-Fourques on the D582 and then pick up the D26 going west in the direction of Brionne. After half a mile on your right you will see the farm on the outskirts of Le Buhot where the SS laagered (**GPS 49.206964, 0.786750**). The woods to the north was where the firefight erupted between the Nazis and the three SAS men in which Bintley was killed and Erlis captured. There is a track that leads north from the road into the woods. As farmer Bardel explained in his written statement to the SAS in 1945, he was forced to bury the Englishman in a refuse pit close to the farm. However, he added, 'eight days after, when the Allies arrived and we were liberated, I disinterred the corpse of Bintley, placed it in a coffin, and then made a grave by the courtyard at the entrance to the wood where he was killed.'

Looking north-east across Le Buhot. The wood (*centre*) in the distance was the scene of the SAS contact with the SS.

The SS laagered in the farmyard of Le Buhot farm, seen here in 2020, and Thomas Bintley was killed in the woods behind.

Brionne

After the war Bintley was disinterred for a second time, but before visiting his final resting place one should visit Brionne, 3 miles to the west. The town was liberated by the Canadians early in the morning of 25 August but not before it had been attacked by Allied bombers, forcing the inhabitants to take shelter in some caves used for mushroom growing.

In the meantime a small party from the second section of 2SAS involved in Trueform arrived in the town under the command of Corporal Hughes. There was a wooden bridge that spanned the river running through the centre of town (**GPS 49.195736, 0.718923**), built by the Nazis to replace the original that had been destroyed during fighting in June 1940. Hughes wanted to blow the wooden bridge but he had insufficient plastic high explosive, so instead he laid waste to a petrol dump.

Rouen

The body of Harold Erlis was fished out of the river Seine in the autumn of 1944, a considerable distance from where he was captured. He was buried in the village churchyard of Yvette, which today lies 5 miles south of Orly airport to the south of Paris.

He was reinterred after the war in St Sever Cemetery Extension, located on the southern edge of Rouen on the Avenue Pierre Lefrançois (**GPS 49.410542, 1.066174**). Most of the burials here are from the First World War but Erlis lies in Block S, a plot that holds 328 victims of the Second World War.

Three views of the main bridge in Brionne. Clockwise from top left: 1920s, 1940 and 2020.

Bayeux

Erlis's pal, Thomas Bintley, was laid to rest in the Bayeux War Cemetery, the largest Second World War cemetery of Commonwealth soldiers in France, containing 4,648 burials (**GPS 49.274112, −0.714339**). Also interred here is James Wilkinson, killed on 5 August during Operation Defoe.

Opposite the cemetery, across a road, is the Bayeux Memorial, which commemorates nearly 2,000 casualties of the battle for Normandy who have no known grave. Twenty-one of the names inscribed on the starkly eloquent memorial are soldiers from 1SAS, killed on the night of 18 June 1944 when their four-engined Short Stirling aircraft, nicknamed 'Yorkshire Rose', taking them to reinforce Operation Houndsworth was lost. Wreckage of the aircraft was never found, although in 2016 an amateur archaeologist claimed he had located its remains in a field in Calvados. This has never been officially verified.

The grave of Thomas Bintley in Bayeux war cemetery.

Chapter Two

Operation Dingson

The two French regiments of the SAS Brigade fought with a singular ferocity upon their return to their homeland in the summer of 1944, but before describing some of their operations, a potted history of their contribution to the SAS is in order.

A detachment of approximately ten officers and forty men under the command of Captain Georges Bergé was posted to Kabrit in January 1942, whereupon the men were incorporated into David Stirling's L Detachment. Weeks earlier, on the inaugural SAS operation, thirty-four of the fifty-five men who had parachuted into Libya to attack enemy airfields had been killed or captured, and Stirling was now desperate for experienced soldiers.

For the next year the French contingent was an integral part of L Detachment, helping it evolve from a small commando unit into the 1st SAS Regiment. However, that expansion, which occurred in September 1942, had a detrimental effect on the French soldiers, as did the capture of Stirling in January 1943. In the subsequent months the SAS was reorganised and the French soldiers were shipped back to England for further training. By now their ranks had swollen with many Frenchmen recruited following the Allied victory in North Africa, and among their number were some soldiers who had served in the Vichy army before switching allegiance.

The French were stationed initially in Camberley, south of London, and it was not a congenial experience. Towards the end of 1943 Captain Carol Mather, who had served in the SAS throughout 1942 and knew several of the Gallic Old Hands, was attached as a liaison officer. He was therefore well acquainted with their strengths as guerrilla soldiers. 'They were found to have many fine qualities and a flair for certain types of operation, and this flair was exploited by us,' he wrote. 'But at the same time it was found necessary to nurse them into operations and by the careful and tactful handling of their patrols, it was found in some cases that they produced even better results than British soldiers.'

Mather was instructed to submit a report on the state of the French volunteers, which he did on 22 December 1943 from their new base in Cupar, on the east coast of Scotland. At the time the French were in three squadrons, commanded by Captain Gualberto Larralde, Lieutenant Pierre Leblond and Lieutenant Pierre Marienne. The squadrons under Larralde and Marienne

Pierre Marienne, seen here during a training exercise in Scotland in 1944, was an admired officer.

were the least experienced, although Mather rated the former 'the fittest squadron'. Marienne's squadron had not yet completed parachute training but the men were 'young and keen'.

Leblond's squadron was the most experienced and most of the men had seen action with the SAS in North Africa. 'They are extremely bitter about having been withdrawn from active operations in the M.E. [Middle East] and dumped in Camberley to vegetate, with no one apparently looking after their interests, and no glimmer of hope of fighting again in a British unit, which is their ideal,' wrote Mather. Demoralised and lacking motivation, they had as a consequence let themselves go. 'Squadron discipline is poor,' noted Mather. 'They are not smart and not particularly clean. Apart from one individual troop, the Squadron seems to have little cohesion ... but I know that this Squadron has great capabilities. Many of the officers and men have carried out missions which demand the highest degrees of endurance, courage and efficiency. All they need is a standard to work up to.'

Mather sympathised with the French. Larralde's squadron, No. 1, was housed in Nissen huts but Nos 2 and 3 had 'extremely bad billets in Cupar town, with sanitary arrangements which are almost non-existent'. This had to be rectified as a matter of urgency, as did the general organisation of the

French squadrons. What the men wanted, reported Mather (and most of the officers), was 'to come on to an SAS footing ... working with British SAS Regts under British direction and organisation. They are quite definite about this. They say that they do not want to be part of a French army, but wish to be Frenchmen working within British units'.

In conclusion, wrote Mather, 'under the present organisation this B [battalion] will not be fit for battle, either as a whole or by Squadrons, by D.Day. The inefficiency of this system will destroy all the keenness and enthusiasm which I know the Squadrons possess.' Mather then advanced his theory as to how to maximise the enormous potential of the French: first, weed out the physically and psychologically unsuitable, and form the remainder into two squadrons who 'should go to the 1st SAS Regt. and to the 2nd SAS Regt. to train and work with them'.

There was much food for thought in the four page report that Mather submitted to 21 Army Group and the French were indeed formed into two entities, the 3rd and 4th Regiments, but they were not mentored by their British counterparts. Instead they were posted to a new training centre at Auchinleck, the 3rd commanded by Pierre Chateau-Jobert and the 4th by Pierre Bourgoin.

Philippe Fauquet and Pierre Marienne (*in the middle of the front row*) parachuted into Brittany in June 1944 but neither survived the war.

The 36-year-old Bourgoin, a big-game hunter before the war, was a veteran warrior who had been wounded four times in three years of fighting, most recently in an aerial attack by a Nazi fighter in Algeria that left him with no fewer than thirty-seven injuries, one of which required the amputation of his right arm. He was considered the ideal man to restore discipline to the experienced French soldiers whose morale had been eroded since returning to Europe.

One such soldier was Corporal Roger Boutinot, an original member of the French detachment which had joined the SAS at Kabrit in January 1942. 'I was very fed up and went to see Bourgoin and I said "I've just come from Africa and I don't want any more of this training. I'm fed up",' he recalled. 'They were all new parachutists and it was like the regular army; every morning you paraded. Bourgoin put me in the officers' mess and I looked after them. My friends were the ones from Kabrit. It was a little group and we stayed together. I didn't bother with the rest of them. Of course, it was because I considered that the new ones who joined [the SAS] only did so after the Americans landed in Algeria and they had to.'

Although it was decided not to have the British SAS regiments mentor their French comrades, there was a recognition that they would benefit from British training officers. One of those attached to the French in early 1944 was Captain Tony Greville-Bell of 2SAS, who had recently recovered from a rib injury sustained on operations in Italy. 'At the start of 1944 I was in charge of a training squadron for the 3 and 4 French,' he recalled. 'I found the French recruits very good indeed; very bright and intelligent and much better educated than the British equivalents and so more easily able to learn. They were very aggressive and their discipline was savage. A lot of officers were former Foreign Legion, and officers struck the men. I don't think they were supposed to but they used to flog them.'

The two French regiments were incorporated into the SAS Brigade, formed in early 1944 on the return to Britain from Italy of the two British regiments under the command of Brigadier Roderick McLeod. 'The French were "formidable",' he reflected. 'The powers that be, in their wisdom, had put the two battalions [sic] into one hutted camp in which the cookhouse, messes, etc., were all shared … the two units did not mix easily.'

McLeod had a high regard for Bourgoin, describing him as 'very tough', and his character rubbed off on his men. 'It was difficult to persuade these splendid characters that the local salmon river should not be used as a grenade range,' wrote McLeod, who also had to smooth ruffled feathers after the French demolished a section of the railway line in the course of practising their sabotage skills with plastic explosives. 'Relations between my HQ and HQ Scottish Command were sometimes very strained. But they certainly did their stuff when they got back into France and I could not have wished for more loyal support.'

In May the French left Scotland for Fairford in Gloucestershire. Anticipation and excitement coursed through the men. 'Each day we waited, confident, playing football, basketball, wrestling,' recalled one officer. 'We were like kids in the playground'.

The 4th Regiment, which contained the desert veterans, was given the honour of leading the French SAS to France. Their general instructions were:

(a) The severance of communications between Brittany and the rest of France in order to prevent reinforcements located in the province from coming to the assistance of enemy troops engaged in the beach-head area.

(b) The recruiting, arming and organising of resistance elements in Brittany, in conjunction with representatives of SHFQ.

There were three operations for 4SAS, Samwest in northern Brittany, Dingson in the south and Cooney. The latter mission, which was launched on 7/8 June, entailed fifty-four men inserted in eighteen three-man teams to cut rail communications throughout the region in which an estimated 150,000 Germans were stationed.

We shall focus on Dingson but, as it loosely overlapped with Samwest, it is worth first sketching an outline of Samwest. On the night of 5/6 June eighteen men under the command of Lieutenants Deschamps and Botella parachuted into a remote area approximately 35 miles west of Saint-Brieuc. Four nights later they were reinforced by Captain Pierre Leblond and around a hundred men, including a Jedburgh team of three. Leblond was perturbed by what he found. Some of the SAS soldiers, ecstatic at being 'home', had let their guard down and were inviting locals to their hideout. 'I gave strict orders to forbid sightseers access to the base, but these orders were indifferently carried out as the paratroopers tended to fraternize with all the world, without distinction or mistrust.'

On 11 June Leblond executed two civilians – a man and a woman – he suspected of being Nazi stooges. The woman was shot, the man despatched with a knife. A few hours later two SAS soldiers chanced upon a German patrol as they went in search of firewood, and this encounter was the spark of a conflagration that swept the SAS base the next day as hundreds of Germans attacked. The French, with the assistance of the Maquis, repelled the first assaults but, as more German reinforcements arrived, Leblond instructed his men to disperse in small parties and make their way on foot 70 miles south to the Dingson base. An estimated 155 Germans were killed in the fighting, while the French losses were thirty-two, five of whom were SAS soldiers. Two, Marcel Ruelle and Daniel Taupin, were caught and thrown into a barn that was then burned to the ground.

Operation Dingson had also been launched on the night of 5/6 June and, like Samwest, the advance party comprised two sticks of eighteen men, one of

Samwest: André Bernard and Francis Folin with Marie Bourne of the Resistance near Trégadoret.

them led by Lieutenant Pierre Marienne and the other by Lieutenant Henri Deplante. Marienne was in his mid-30s, described as an intellectual, with a love of poetry and literature. Born in Algeria, he had been captured in 1940 during the battle for France, but leapt from the POW train taking him to Germany. He made his way to Algeria with the intention of reaching Gibraltar but was arrested by the Vichy police and sentenced to death. The Allied invasion of North Africa came just in time for Marienne and he was released in November 1942. He arrived in England in the spring of 1943 and joined the French SAS in Camberley.

Marienne's stick landed on French soil at 0045 hours on 6 June, a mile east of the hamlet of Halliguen and 2 miles from the intended DZ. The eight SAS soldiers and one SOE agent swiftly found one another. It seemed like a perfect insertion. But it wasn't. Their descent had been seen by a German observation post sited in a windmill half a mile east from the spot where they had landed.

Marienne left four men close to their DZ, three of whom were wireless operators, while he and the rest of the party went to search for Deplante's section. Minutes after their departure, a company of Georgian Nazis arrived. The SAS exchanged fire and Corporal Émile Bouétard was hit in the shoulder. He and his comrades continued the fight until their ammunition ran out, by which time they had destroyed their radio and code books. The wounded Bouétard was executed by the Georgians, who would have shot the other three Frenchmen but for the intervention of their German officer. The trio,

Pierre Etrich, Louis Jourdan and Maurice Sauvé, all survived captivity, which was unusual for French SAS personnel.

Marienne had heard the commotion and made a rapid assessment. There was no point joining the fray; it was evident that the enemy had arrived in force. He must press on to fulfil his mission.

Lieutenant Henri Deplante and his section had landed 5 miles away from their DZ and it wasn't until dawn on 7 June that they reached the rendezvous point at the Kergonan bridge. There was no sign of Marienne so Deplante established a base in the Donnan forest, a quarter of a mile from the bridge, and radioed a message to England.

Marienne in the meanwhile had made an important discovery. A farmer close to the village of Plaudren had sheltered him and his men, and put the SAS officer in contact with the local Maquis group, whose HQ was in a farm called La Nouette, 1½ miles west of the village of Saint-Marcel, whose occupant, Monsieur Pondard, was delighted to do his bit. Just north-west of the farm was a field, codenamed *Baleine* (whale), which since May 1943 had received thirty resupplies by air. Encircled by trees and hedgerows, and at some distance from the road, the field was an ideal DZ.

As a result La Nouette was the HQ for all the Maquis groups in southern Brittany and since the broadcast of a codeword on 4 June by the BBC all the fighters had assembled primed to wage a guerrilla war against the Occupiers.

Marienne had known nothing of this prior to his arrival in Brittany but he saw the sense in establishing Dingson's base close to La Nouette, particularly as there was an existing DZ close by. The two SAS sticks were reunited on the evening of 7 June and Marienne radioed a message to Colonel Bourgoin at SAS HQ informing him of their situation and the 'immense possibilities' for a guerrilla campaign.

On 9 June Brigadier Rory McLeod issued a communique to Colonel Bourgoin, shortly before he flew from England to parachute onto the *Baleine* DZ, assuring him that 21 Army Group 'have decided that as soon as possible everything will be done to encourage a large scale revolt in Brittany'. This included the supply of arms and equipment to the combined French force.

Once Bourgoin had dropped into Dingson's base he took stock of the situation and radioed to England a shopping list:

Bren light machine gun	400
Rifle	1,000
Discharger cup (for rifle)	150
Mortar, 3-inch	100
PIAT	100
Rifle sniper	100

The RAF appeared on consecutive nights, their largest drop happening on 14/15 June when twenty-five Stirling bombers guided by the Eureka/Rebecca

The *Baleine* DZ north-west of La Nouette in 2021, and Resistance fighters collecting containers dropped in June 1944.

transponding radar deposited 780 containers on the *Baleine* DZ, each one weighing on average 200kg. Inside was everything from arms to medical supplies to flour, so the Maquis baker could bake baguettes.

Four days later four jeeps were safely parachuted in, although the container with the vehicles' Vickers machine guns smashed on landing and three-quarters of the weapons were irreparably damaged.

Word spread of the arsenal being assembled at La Nouette and more volunteers arrived to offer their services, emboldened also by news of the Normandy landings. The SAS were soon reporting by wireless potential targets for Allied aircraft; a radio station was destroyed and on 16 June a German HQ in a local château received a direct hit from an American P-47 Thunderbolt, resulting in a large fire and many deaths.

Bourgoin and the SAS also started to train their callow but enthusiastic countrymen preparatory to embarking on a guerrilla campaign, but his plans were derailed by an incident on the night of 17 June. Five RAF aircraft on another resupply mission dropped their cargo on to what they assumed were the DZ illuminations at *Baleine* but were in fact the village lights of Le-Roc-Saint-André, 5 miles to the north. The 120 containers that landed proved to

A photo taken from the ground by French SAS showing the RAF delivering vital supplies.

the Germans that close at hand must be a large enemy base. On that same evening Bourgoin received a message from Brigadier McLeod informing him that the breakout from the beachhead at Normandy had stalled and therefore the Dingson base was to disperse and begin attacking the enemy transport and lines of communication forthwith. He also ordered Bourgoin to 'avoid at all cost a pitched battle'.

Captain Pierre Leblond reached the Dingson base at 0300 hours on 18 June. He was impressed with what he found. Captain Gualberto Larralde led the 'Larralde battalion', composed of one 4SAS squadron and around 900 Maquis, positioned to the east and north-east of the base close to the farm of Le Bois Joly and the manor house at Sainte-Geneviève; the 'Caro battalion' faced north and west and was composed of 700 Maquis and a handful of SAS soldiers, and the 700-strong 'Le Garrec battalion' was commanded by Lieutenant Marienne and was dug in to the south and south-east. In addition, several units were still in the process of being organised and there was also a company of gendarmes. Situated in La Nouette farmhouse was the HQ, which contained a 'considerable liaison staff, mostly women [and] a score of motor cars'. There was also a field kitchen, a first aid post and an admin-istration section for food, arms and ammunition. In total there were sixteen 4SAS officers and 171 troops within the Saint-Marcel camp.

Not long after dawn broke on 18 June (eyewitness accounts as to when the shooting started vary between 0430 and 0500 hours), two Citroën Traction Avants, the executive black automobiles favoured by both the Resistance and the Gestapo, appeared on the road that skirted the southern perimeter of the French base. They were heading east towards Saint-Marcel. The eight German military policemen inside the vehicles had no idea they were approaching a sprawling enemy camp, although they were probably aware that a few hours earlier a large quantity of containers had been dropped at Le-Roc-Saint-André.

The Germans might have been on the lookout for signs of Maquis activity; instead they were ambushed by a section of Lieutenant Marienne's SAS on a bend in the road. The first burst of machine-gun fire shattered the windscreen of the leading vehicle, wounding two of the four occupants. In the next moment a shell from the PIAT hit the second Citroën head on, killing all those inside. The first car accelerated round the bend but came under more fire. The Germans stumbled out of their vehicle and two were shot dead. A third was captured but the fourth managed to dart into the trees and evade capture. Villagers in Saint-Marcel observed the startled German running through the streets, threatening to shoot anyone he saw with his MP40 (Schmeisser) submachine gun. At around 0600 hours he reached the 500-strong German garrison at Malestroit, 2 miles east of Saint-Marcel. On hearing his tale, the commander mobilised two companies with the intention of eliminating what he assumed was a small but well-armed local Maquis group.

A young farmhand in the fields saw the Germans arrive in Saint-Marcel on foot around 0900 hours. He ran the half mile west to the hamlet of Les Hardys-Béhélec to warn the soldiers dug-in in gun pits sited at 10-yard intervals along the southern and western perimeter of the camp. The French had just returned to their positions after a Sunday Mass, conducted by the priest of Saint-Marcel, Abbé Le Nueff, under a parachute canopy rigged between some trees. 'One should not talk of vengeance but of revenge,' he told his congregation. 'They have won the first set but we, with the help of God, will win the second. Go and prepare for combat.'

Minutes after the Mass had ended, the Germans launched their attack at the strongest point of the French camp, the hinge in the south-east sector between Lieutenant Marienne's battalion and Captain Larralde's. Here were SAS soldiers, well-armed and itching for a fight. They watched the Germans striding through the fields in the pale morning sunshine and then opened fire. 'They were repulsed without too much trouble,' recalled Leblond. 'But it was necessary to send the Gendarme Company to back up the SE side and then some FFI elements to help Larralde.'

Beaten back, the German survivors waited in Saint-Marcel for reinforcements. Now they understood that this was clearly more than just a small, skilled Maquis group. When more troops had arrived from Malestroit, the Nazis probed north-west towards the farm at Le Bois Joly, suspecting this was where the Maquis HQ was based. They advanced across sloping fields abundant with wheat, while others moved silently up a sunken lane, the hedgerows and thickly leaved trees concealing their presence.

Less than 100 metres from the farm at Le Bois Joly was a Maquis outpost. Among the five Frenchmen on sentry duty there were two cousins, Paul and Jean Le Blavec, aged 20 and 22. They were taken by surprise when the Germans attacked. The fight was brief. The Frenchmen – one of whom was SAS soldier Daniel Casa – were all killed, and in the crossfire a bullet fatally wounded a 14-year-old girl (some reports gave her age as 15), Suzanne Berthelot, who was tending her cattle in the field just beyond the outpost. She was a Parisienne who had been sent by her family to the countryside because they believed it would be safer.

Having seized the farm buildings at Le Bois Joly, the Germans advanced towards the large manor house at Sainte-Geneviève, a quarter of a mile north. Still living in the house were the occupants, Madame Andrée Bouvard and her six children. Her absent husband Michel was a high-ranking air force officer.

The eldest child, 15-year-old Loïc, had successfully badgered the SAS for an American carbine and now joined in the defence of his home (for which he was awarded the Croix de Guerre). Michel, aged 13, acted as a runner, passing messages from the SAS command post in Sainte-Geneviève to the various sections dug in around the buildings, while the youngest boy,

11-year-old Philippe, repeatedly used his knowledge of the terrain to crawl out into No Man's Land and bring back reports about the disposition of the German forces. The Bren guns dropped by air at the request of Colonel Bourgoin took a heavy toll on the Germans, as did the Vickers on Lieutenant Marienne's jeep. The other SAS vehicles were used to transport the wounded from Sainte-Geneviève to the aid post at La Nouette.

Fresh German soldiers arrived, including elements from the elite 2nd Parachute Division, and a new onslaught was launched against the eastern sector. In the early afternoon Captain Larralde ordered his dwindling force to withdraw half a mile after their mortar teams were overrun. Bourgoin ordered every available man at HQ to bolster Larralde's forces, who were bearing the brunt of the Nazi offensive. The colonel also radioed HQ and requested an air strike on 'lorried infantry'. Seventy minutes later, at 1330 hours, a squadron of P-47s arrived and although they saw no movement on the roads, they strafed a train and several Nazi units in and around Saint-Marcel, which had 'a big morale effect on the ground'.

The Germans reorganised themselves and in the late afternoon made another thrust at the southern and eastern sectors. A large contingent of FFI under the command of Captain Cosquer were housed in the Château Béhélec, armed with Brens and mortars, whose 'relentless resistance' defied several German attempts to storm the elegant building. In the surrounding woods around the hamlet of Les Hardys-Béhélec there was bitter hand-to-hand fighting between the French and the Nazis.

Further north the Germans renewed their assault on Sainte-Geneviève, a battalion of Georgians spearheading the offensive. They eliminated two Bren gun positions and reached the wall surrounding the manor house, but the weight of fire from the building halted any further progress. Le Bois Joly, which had been recaptured by the French earlier in the afternoon, once again fell to the Germans. Marienne directed his men to withdraw 300 metres to the west where they formed a new defensive line.

Slowly the French camp was shrinking and casualties were mounting: six SAS soldiers and thirty-six Maquis had been killed, with a further sixty wounded. The German casualties were many and hundreds of corpses littered the fields and woods.

The final attack of the day came at 2000 hours when the Germans attempted to push further north through Les Hardys-Béhélec but the French line, marshalled by Marienne, held firm and the Bren guns scythed them down. 'During these counter-attacks Jeeps were used with gratifying effect on the enemy's flanks,' reported Leblond.

Not long after nightfall Bourgoin gathered his officers and the Maquis leaders in the HQ at La Nouette. It had, wrote Leblond, 'become clear that the enemy was present in strength and that it would be impossible to hold on much longer without entirely exhausting our ammunition'. It was expected that the next morning German armour would arrive.

Bourgoin explained how the withdrawal would be managed. First to leave would be the motor transport convoy, making for Trédion, 10 miles to the west. Next would be the Caro Battalion, heading 15 miles north to Josselin. Larralde's Battalion would withdraw 75 miles north-west to Callac, and last to leave would be Marienne's Battalion, which was also to regroup at Trédion. On reaching their destinations the battalions were to disperse, with the Maquis returning to their home areas to await further orders. Bourgoin instructed the SAS to 'lie low for about ten days and then we will begin sabotaging'.

The withdrawal began not long after nightfall at around 2200 hours, the French slipping away to the north and west without incident, despite Leblond's assessment that 'orderliness and discipline were not of the best'. A couple of hours before the French began to disperse, the German 2nd Parachute Division had launched yet another attack at the Château Béhélec in the southern sector but without success. The enemy, remarked an officer, was still 'dogged and tenacious'. In a report to the 2nd Parachute Division's commanding officer, General Hermann-Bernhard Ramcke, it was stated that when the attack was recommenced at first light on 19 June, the Germans discovered that 'the enemy had evacuated the position during the night or in the early hours and had withdrawn towards the north-west. A reconnaissance that was launched immediately had found no trace [of the enemy] up until this moment ... we have recovered a large quantity of explosives, weapons and parachute material.'

Enraged that their enemy had slipped from their grasp, and that an esti-mated 560 of their soldiers had been killed, the Nazis embarked on an orgy of violence led by the Georgian troops. The château was razed, along with several houses in Les Hardys-Béhélec, but the Germans wanted more. They dragged 31-year-old Felix Guil from his house and shot him in front of his wife. A similar fate befell 83-year-old Madame Le Blanc, who was blind, murdered in her bed, and her terrified grandson, 15-year-old Yves Ayoul, shot as he cowered under a table. Two wounded SAS soldiers, Jean Vasseur and Gaston Navailles, were discovered sheltering in houses in the days after the battle, and summarily executed.

Colonel Bourgoin established a new HQ at La Foliette, 8 miles west of Saint-Marcel, and Captain Leblond acted as his adjutant, handing over command of his No. 2 squadron to Lieutenant François Martin, one of the desert veterans who had joined the SAS in 1942. 'We spent this time in trying to find out where the paratroops were, and sending liaison officers to them,' noted Leblond, who was subsequently awarded a Military Cross for his 'great initiative and self-reliance'. Another pressing task was to treat the wounded, around fifty in total, of whom nineteen were in a grave state. Lieutenant

Marienne took up this responsibility, driving them in a convoy to a large rambling country house at Lizio, a couple of miles from the command post at La Foliette. Here lived two young women, Henriette and Amelie, who allowed their house to be transformed into a hospital.

By the end of the month most of 4SAS had congregated on a new base, codenamed Grog, close to Pontivy, 20 miles north-west of Saint-Marcel. Resupplies were dropped and at the start of July they began what would be a successful guerrilla war against the Germans. Nonetheless there was a concerted effort by the Nazis to track down the saboteurs who caused them such carnage. As well as infantry units, they were assisted by the Abwehr, the intelligence wing of the Wehrmacht, and some Milice, the French fascist paramilitary unit.

Lieutenant Marienne and his section kept constantly on the move, never resting long in the isolated farmhouses they used as brief bases. On 10 July he and his men arrived at the hamlet of Kérihuel, which the local Maquis judged more secure than their previous lodgings. They were mistaken. Somewhere along the line there was an informer, and shortly before dawn on 12 July Marienne and his men were surrounded by a significant force of Nazis. The eighteen Frenchmen were ordered to lie on the ground face down. Marienne was shot first in the back of the head, then François Martin and the five other SAS soldiers, and finally the eight FFI and three locals accused of aiding the 'terrorists', as the Nazis called them. So sudden had the Nazi attack been that Marienne had not had time to destroy his notebook in which were written details of arms caches and the names of trusted locals to whom he could go for food. In the days that followed several brave Frenchmen and women were executed as the Nazis toured the area with Marienne's notebook as their guide.

Nevertheless throughout July and into August 4SAS and a 3SAS operation in the north of Brittany, codenamed Derry, organised and trained a formidable FFI army, while also harassing the Germans and cutting their lines of communications. Other 3SAS parties were dropped further south into France with instructions to kill as many of the enemy as possible as they withdrew towards Germany. They carried out their orders with ardour, killing an estimated 2,340 Germans and wounding nearly 3,000 between 16 July and 7 October.

4SAS also moved further south following the breakout of the Americans in Normandy in late July, and on 29 August the entire regiment, 300 men in fifty jeeps, launched Operation Spencer, the objective of which was to prevent the Germans moving north-east as the Allies advanced from the south of France by blocking the Loire east of Bourges. 4SAS achieved outstanding results, taking 2,500 prisoners and persuading a further 20,000 Germans to surrender to the Americans.

Colonel Pierre-Louis Bourgoin (*centre*) at the liberation of Vannes on 4 August 1944.

But it was in Brittany where 4SAS made their most important contribution to the liberation of their country. It came at a cost – the loss of sixty-five soldiers, twenty-five of whom were executed after capture – but their work had not gone unnoticed. In his report of the invasion of France, General Dwight Eisenhower, supreme commander of SHAEF, praised the 'ceaseless harassing activities' of 4SAS and their Maquis allies in Brittany who 'surrounded the Germans with a terrible atmosphere of danger and hatred which ate into the confidence of the leaders and courage of their soldiers'.

On 12 September 1944 Lieutenant Colonel Morice (real name Paul Chenailler), commanding FFI in the Morbihan department of western Brittany, wrote a letter of appreciation to Brigadier McLeod. 'Thank you for the generous help which you have given to my Bns [battalions] since D day,' said Morice. 'As a result of your kindness, by the intermediary of OC 4 French Para Bn, 10,000 men have been armed in my Department. I can confirm that my men have shown that they merit your confidence, more than 5,000 prisoners have been taken, at least as many enemy have been killed and large amounts of material captured … the French of Morbihan will never forget what they owe to their British friends.'

Visiting Operation Dingson and the Battle of Saint-Marcel

Le Halliguen

It is logical to start any pilgrimage of Brittany at the spot where Lieutenant Pierre Marienne and his eight men landed not long after midnight on 6 June 1944. A memorial to the first SAS soldier killed in France, Émile Bouétard, stands on a lane called Le Halliguen (**GPS 47.837377, –2.659612**), between the hamlet of the same name to the west and the town of Plumelec (pronounced Plume-e-leck) to the east. An information board, in French, stands close by the memorial, and an arrow marks the spot where Bouétard was killed, approximately 100 metres north of the monument.

Bouétard was an interesting character, a sailor since the age of 13, who after the capitulation of France in 1940 worked for eighteen months as a farmhand in his native Brittany. He eventually made it to Britain in January 1943 and enlisted in the SAS. On 23 October 1943 he was among a team of French paratroopers who set a new world speed record for a stick jump, twenty men jumping from a Douglas aircraft in seven-and-a-half seconds, landing within a DZ of 389 metres. The previous record had been set by US airborne forces.

Marienne and his men were spotted descending by a German observation point situated in a windmill half a mile east from where they had landed. That windmill, the moulin de La Grée, still stands and forms part of an elaborate and poignant memorial to the French SAS.

The memorial stone for Émile Bouétard. The row of trees 100 metres behind marks the approximate spot where he was killed.

The record-breaking French parachute team of 1943, including Bouétard (*back row, fifth from the right*) and Marienne (*front row, seventh from the left*).

Plumelec

The memorial (**GPS 47.832437, –2.643356**) is approximately a mile south of Plumelec and is signposted 'Mémorial des parachutistes SAS'. There is parking next to the windmill. By the windmill is a large plaque on which there is a potted history of the French SAS, and 20 metres away is the centrepiece of the memorial. Designed in 1989 by the sculptor Jean Mélinard, himself an SAS veteran, it is a long wall on which are thirty-nine Crosses of Lorraine – the emblem of the FFI – and on which are engraved the names of the seventy-seven French SAS soldiers who were killed during operations in Brittany in 1944.

In front of the wall is a large flat granite stone emblazoned in metal with the SAS flaming sword of Excalibur and the regiment's legendary motto 'Who Dares Win'. Underneath is another plaque in French, on which is written: 'To the French SAS who gave their lives in Brittany for the liberation of France – 5 June to August 1944.'

Pierre Bourgoin, the commanding officer of 4SAS, survived the war and died in 1970 at the aged of 62. His grave is only a mile from the SAS memorial in the cemetery of Plumelec (**GPS 47.838034, –2.642284**). There is plenty of parking in the town centre (and a good selection of cafés and restaurants). Enter the cemetery by the gate on the Rue Martyrs de la Résistance, and Bourgoin's grave is at the front of the cemetery, against the wall on the right-hand side.

On the other side of the cemetery wall from Bourgoin's grave is a large crucifixion cross, behind which are four slabs bearing the names of the town's civilian victims of the war. Also here, to the left of the cross, is the grave of Pierre Marienne (and also an inscription on the right of the cross commemorating François Martin, who was executed with Marienne but who is buried in his home town cemetery of Hardricourt, just north of Paris). A street in Plumelec bears Marienne's name, as does one in the coastal town of Lorient.

Close to Marienne's grave is a large information board, La Voie De La Liberation (The road of Liberation), which explains that Plumelec was liberated on 6 August 1944 by the 4th US Armored Division commanded by General John Shirley Wood. The square outside the cemetery is the Place du Colonel Bourgoin, and in the middle is a 15ft menhir, erected in 1971, shortly after Bourgoin's death. A plaque explains that it was erected to 'perpetuate the memory' of the resistance of the Maquis and the SAS.

All these sites were included in a two-day commemoration by the French military in June 2019 to coincide with the 75th anniversary of the Normandy landings. The occasion concluded with a parachute demonstration over the Vannesd-Meucon aerodrome by members of the 1st Marine Infantry Parachute Regiment, the successors of the French SAS.

The SAS memorial at Plumelec. The names of the dead are engraved on the crosses of Lorraine.

Marienne memorial

Marienne and Martin were initially buried just to the north of where they were shot on the morning of 12 July, behind the farm of Alexandre Gicquello, who lived in Kérihuel and had aided the SAS. He and his 18-year-old son Remy were also executed with the soldiers, along with a third villager, Fernand Danet.

The site of their execution at Kérihuel (**GPS 47.811478, –2.672715**) is 7 miles south of Plumelec. Take the D126 to Cadoudal before turning right onto Le Guer d'en Bas and you will soon see three flags fluttering on their poles – the French Tricolore, the American Stars and Stripes and the black and white stripes of the Breton Gwenn-ha-du.

A large stone cross marks the spot where the eighteen men were made to lie on the ground before being shot, and on the wall behind – a reconstruction of the original – are the names of the dead engraved on three plaques.

The death of Lieutenant François Martin was a terrible blow for 4SAS. He was the most experienced SAS officer in the two French regiments, a man who had first seen action in the Norwegian campaign in April 1940. He was one of the first officers to rally to Charles de Gaulle after the fall of France in June that year and he was a training officer for the FFL (Forces françaises libres) when they began arriving in England in the summer of 1940. Shipped to the Middle East in October 1941, Martin joined the SAS in 1942 and participated in several operations, including the jeep raid on Sidi Haneish airfield in July 1942 that accounted for eighteen German planes.

The execution site at Kérihuel in 1944 and ...

... the execution site in 2021.

The Battle of Saint-Marcel

From the site of their execution to the battlefield where Martin and Marienne had marshalled their forces so adroitly is approximately 15 miles east on the D10.

There is much to visit at Saint-Marcel and the logical place to begin is the excellent Resistance Museum (**GPS 47.804263, –2.431911**). Initially inaugurated in 1984, the museum underwent an extensive two-year renovation and reopened in September 2021 in a ceremony attended by 96-year-old Marcel Bergamasco, believed to be the last survivor of the Battle of Saint-Marcel. He was a driver for the Maquis and during the battle transported the wounded to the first aid post and ferried ammunition to the front line.

Spread over 1,600 square metres, the interactive museum houses over a thousand artefacts, including a Willys jeep, as used by the SAS, a wedding dress made from an SAS parachute silk, and many vehicles, uniforms and weapons. As well as explaining the events of June 1944, the museum also sheds light on what life was like for Bretons during the long and bitter years of Nazi Occupation.

The museum is open all year except January. For more information visit: www.musee-resistance-bretagne.com.

The Memorial Trail

You can drive or walk from the museum at Saint-Marcel to Le Bois Joly as part of a 3-mile tour of the battlefield called the 'Memorial Trail', which was officially launched in 2020. The trail encompasses eleven markers, branded with the red Cross of Lorraine, at sites significant to the Battle of Saint-Marcel. It is possible to complete the trail by car (or bicycle) but on foot is particularly rewarding as it gives one a greater sense of the terrain, which has changed little in over three-quarters of a century. The narrow path that leads from the museum to the farm at Bois Joly is, in season, overhung with leafy branches and bordered by hedgerows, and one can understand how the Germans made use of the natural surroundings to approach unseen towards the French outposts.

Marker 1: The Museum

Marker 2 (**GPS 47.804351, −2.429440**)
The location of the prominent marker board complete with route map and explanation (in French).

Markers 3 and 4 (**GPS 47.808123, −2.426863**)
These markers are situated 50 metres from the present-day Bois Joly farm, scene of some heavy fighting throughout 18 June. A menhir engraved with the names of six French people (including the adolescent farmhand Suzanne Berthelot) stands close to the spot where the FFI outpost was attacked on the morning of the battle. An information board close by in French explains the sequence of events that day.

Markers 5, 6, 7 and 8 (**GPS 47.803918, −2.418625**)
These markers are situated in the village of Saint-Marcel. Marker 5 commemorates the sacrifice of the village, officially designated a 'Martyr Village' for what it suffered in 1944. It is one of the few villages to be awarded the Croix de Guerre with Palm for its collective resistance under the Nazi yoke.

The memorial at Bois Joly looking north towards the house on the site where the farm stood.

Marker 6 is a memorial that honours six villagers who were executed in the wake of the Battle of Saint-Marcel, and whose remains were only located in the 1960s.

Marker 7 is a memorial in recognition of three villagers who were deported to concentration camps during the war: Suzanne Bouvard-Latapie, Annic Philouze and Eugène Fablet. Annic and Suzanne were cousins and during the Battle of Saint-Marcel they were in the first aid post treating the wounded SAS and FFI. They slipped away from the battlefield along with the rest of the French during the night of 18/19 June, and made it on foot to the village of Malestroit, but they were arrested the next day as they returned to Saint-Marcel to collect their bicycles. Interrogated and beaten, they were deported to Ravensbrück concentration camp. Both survived and Annic subsequently became a nun, dying in 2017 aged 99.

Marker 8 is a tribute to Emile Morel, a Resistance fighter from Saint-Marcel who was captured after the battle and executed at Fort Penthièvre on 13 July 1944.

Markers 9, 10 and 11 (**GPS 47.800573, –2.432224**)

These three markers are in the vicinity of Les Hardys-Béhélec, the scene of some of the heaviest fighting on 18 June. Marker 9 marks the spot on what was the farm where on the morning of 19 June the Germans executed three civilians: Felix Guil, Madame Le Blanc and Yves Ayoul. Their photographs adorn an information board close to the memorial stone and there are also interesting photos of the château des Hardys-Béhélec before and after the battle.

The memorial stone at Hardys-Béhélec is close to where three villagers were murdered by the Nazis.

Marker 10 is close to the site of the château des Hardys-Béhélec, which the Germans repeatedly tried without success to capture during the battle. The château was razed by the Nazis on 25 June and was never rebuilt.

Marker 11 is the clearing where, on 27 July 1947, General Charles de Gaulle presided over a ceremony to honour the achievements of the Breton Resistance during the Occupation.

There is plenty of parking, both at the museum and at the Hardys-Béhélec farm shop, which sells a wide range of organic produce, including beer, wine and jam.

Sainte-Geneviève

Just outside the boundary of the Memorial Trail is Sainte-Geneviève (**GPS 47.813188, –2.423730**), approximately a quarter of a mile from Le Bois Joly as the crow flies. To reach the old manor house, where on 18 June Madame Bouvard and her six children aided the SAS and FFI during long hours of fierce fighting, travel east along the lane from the Le Bois Joly markers and then turn left (north) up the road called 'Le Chesnot' until you reach the entrance to Sainte-Geneviève. It is a private residence but from the front entrance one gets a good view of some of the buildings that seventy-five years ago were out-houses to the manor house.

Loïc Bouvard, the 15-year-old who was decorated with a Croix de Guerre for his courage during the defence of his home, enjoyed an illustrious post-war life. After a successful career with Air France, mainly in the USA, he returned to Brittany and in 1973 was elected the region's MP for the centre-right UMP. He held his seat until 2012 and died five years later aged 88.

The Memorial to Breton Resistance

There are several other monuments and sites of interest beyond the remit of the Memorial Trail, and it is most rewarding to discover them. Starting from the Resistance museum, turn left out of the car park and follow the road for just a few metres. The bend in the road (**GPS 47.804034, –2.433603**) is where the SAS ambushed the two Citroens full of military policemen at dawn on 18 June, the opening shots of the Battle of Saint-Marcel.

As you continue west you will pass on your right the farms of Les Petits Hardis and Les Grands Hardys, both of which were occupied by the French during the fighting. The Germans attacked through the fields to your left, and suffered numerous casualties from the SAS Bren guns.

Follow the road as it passes under the N166 and curves left and before you is the Memorial to Breton Resistance (**GPS 47.802539, –2.446034**). The first stone of this stark, domineering memorial was laid by Charles de Gaulle when he visited the scene of the battle in 1947. Four years later the monument was inaugurated in a ceremony attended by General Marie-Pierre Koenig, the wartime commander of the FFI. The monument is in the shape of a lantern with four adjoining Crosses of Lorraine at the top. The marble plaque gives a

The Memorial to Breton Resistance facing La Nouette farm.

brief description of the battle of Saint-Marcel and states that 560 enemy soldiers were killed in the fighting for the loss of forty-two Frenchmen. There is an annual ceremony in June at the memorial to honour the memory of the fallen.

Standing with one's back to the plaque, one is afforded a good view of La Nouette farm, the French HQ during the battle (**GPS 47.804598, –2.448138**). It is possible to walk up the gates of the farm along the track close to the memorial, but to reach the *Baleine* DZ one must go on foot across country. Skirt the edge of the meadow to the left of the lane leading to La Nouette and continue in a north-westerly direction for approximately a quarter of a mile. The field that slopes upwards, encircled on three sides by trees, is the DZ (**GPS 47.805146, –2.453706**). The origin of its name remains a mystery; it has been claimed it was on account of the shape of the field, but others suggest it was chosen because a whale is a beast that inspires admiration and affection among people.

Chapter Three

Operations Hardy and Wallace

Operation Wallace was many months in the planning. In May 1944 it was proposed that an SAS base should be established from D-Day in the Plateau de Langres, a sparsely populated area of eastern France between the Morvan (west) and the Vosges (east). The plateau, mostly thick forests interspersed across undulating countryside, owed its name to the town that was perched on the high point of the region, at approximately 1,800ft, to the west of Dijon. This plan fell through, however, because the Royal Air Force expressed grave reservations about their ability to fly to this area in the limited hours of darkness in June. Political sensitivities were also an issue, and objections were raised about 'uniformed troops being employed there when for the same Air Force reasons it had not been possible to arm FFI (French Forces of the Interior)'.

So Wallace fell into abeyance, to the frustration of the SAS Brigade, and particularly 2SAS, and it was not until 4 July that 21 Army Group approved the insertion of a detachment of soldiers into the Plateau de Langres. The advance party was codenamed Operation Hardy and chosen to lead it was Captain Grant Hibbert. Born in Manchester in 1918, Hibbert had volunteered for 2SAS in 1943 from the Royal Artillery while stationed in Malta, and had proved his mettle with the regiment during operations in Italy. 'He was a very tall thin man with glasses,' recalled Cyril Wheeler, a member of Baobab. 'He was strict and upright ... a good officer, respected.'

The Hardy party emplaned on the night of 26/27 July at the RAF base at Tarrant Rushton in Dorset. There were three sticks of three men in three aircraft, including two signallers and three drivers. Also loaded onto the aircraft were three Willys jeeps, the light utility vehicle that had been a favourite of the SAS since the summer of 1942 in North Africa. Named after its manufacturer Willys Overland (although Ford was also involved in its construction), the jeep was a powerful and versatile four-wheeled drive vehicle with a top speed of 60mph.

For several weeks the RAF had been dropping the jeeps into France where they were gratefully received by SAS parties. The vehicles were transported inside elaborate protective cradles, positioned on a sub-frame with attachment points for steel suspension cables by each wheel. Initially eight standard parachutes (28ft) were attached to each cradle but it was quickly discovered that a safer and more effective way was to use four 60ft parachutes. Before being loaded into the cradles, the jeeps had their windscreen folded down, and the guns and steering wheel stashed safely inside the vehicle. The petrol, gun mountings, tools and spare wheels were delivered from the air in fourteen cylindrical containers.

The plan was for the three parties to parachute into the Morvan, a rugged region in central France, west of the Plateau de Langres, where waiting for them would be men of A Squadron, 1SAS, who since early June had been operating with great success. But the drop did not go according to plan. The jeep from the first plane 'fell without parachutes and became unrecognisable [and] the third party did not drop on account of low cloud conditions obscuring the DZ'. This third plane returned to England, taking with it Lieutenant Hibbert and two men, and command of Hardy temporarily fell to Lieutenant Dayrell Morris, a 31-year-old from Edinburgh. Two 6-pounder field guns (which 1SAS subsequently used to great effect) were also dropped and they came down intact, to the delight of Captain Alex Muirhead, in charge of the 1SAS welcome committee. On the night of 27/28 July Hibbert and his two men were successfully dropped but the two jeeps that accompanied them were not so fortunate. 'Pranged' jeeps, as the SAS called those whose parachutes failed to deploy, were an occupational hazard. A further attempt was made on 30/31 July and this time the two vehicles landed without mishap.

Early on the morning of 1 August the 2SAS party, guided by Sergeant Major Reg Seekings of 1SAS, departed the Morvan for the hamlet of Rolle, 70 miles to the east, a distance they covered in four hours. 'The party kept to small roads and always crossed main roads at a direct crossing,' noted Hibbert. At Rolle the 2SAS detachment was welcomed by another 1SAS contingent, commanded by Captain John Wiseman. For nearly a month he and five men had been observing the German garrison in Dijon, 6 miles to the north-east, frequently calling up air strikes on enemy targets.

A French guide had been organised to lead Hibbert and his men to the Plateau de Langres but he never showed. So, on the evening of 4 August the three 2SAS jeeps set off unaccompanied. It was 50 miles to the southern edge of the plateau, which they reached without incident, but they continued for another 15 miles until they were in the rugged interior of the plateau. At 0530 hours on 5 August they laagered as dawn broke.

They remained concealed for 24 hours and on 6 August Hibbert made a recce on foot and contacted some local farmers, who soon put him in touch with Jean Le Garzac, a member of the local Maquis group, operating from the forests close to the village of Recey-sur-Ource. 'I was somewhat stupefied to see coming towards me a jeep that negotiated the forest tracks as easily as the main roads,' remarked Le Garzac. 'The height, the informality, the friendliness of this officer who got out made me forget all our problems. Hibbert spoke good French, fortunately, because I could only speak a little German.' Le Garzac directed Hibbert to some hidden tracks in the woods, close to Le Petit Saint Broing, and it was here that Hibbert established Base No. 1. Operation Hardy was under way.

On the night of 8/9 August a party of ten reinforcements, led by 20-year-old Lieutenant Alex Robertson, arrived by parachute, and for the next few days Hibbert sent out a series of reconnaissance patrols. They moved to a new base on 12 August because the initial hideout had 'been in an area abounding in grouse and the German officers were said to be fond of hunting in the neighbourhood'. In addition, wild boar were numerous and at night they came close to the camp 'and sounded like Germans'. Eleven more men of C Squadron, 2SAS, parachuted into Hardy's operational area on the night of 15/16 August, and a further five – along with twenty-five containers – arrived on the following evening. The DZ was at La Maison-Neuve, a couple of miles north of Recey-sur-Ource, codenamed 'Bronchite' by the Maquis.

Jean Le Garzac left a vivid description of a parachutage on the night of 23 August, which he called 'one of the most wonderfully intense moments of my life'. Hibbert, he said, 'was an extremely meticulous organiser and his men held him in high regard. He spoke little but when he did, he knew when and what to say. But in spite of his reticence, he possessed a human warmth that I appreciated.'

Le Garzac watched as one of the SAS signallers operated a Eureka/Rebecca transponding radar. Consisting of two parts, the Eureka was a ground-operated transponder, which emitted a single morse letter continuously prior to the expected time of the aircraft's arrival. As the plane approached, the Rebecca transceiver and antenna system on board picked up the ground signal on its radar screen, enabling the pilot to hone in on the DZ.

'Far off we heard a purr, which, little by little, grew louder,' said Le Garzac. 'They're coming! Hibbert was as calm as ever. For him it's a simple manoeuvre, and yet in a moment I would see him spring to life. One aircraft, then a second – their bomb doors open – and a third and a fourth. Parachutes fill the sky and containers begin landing. From the last aircraft jump men.'

There were twenty-four containers in total, and one pannier, along with six soldiers. One of the men seemed to be descending onto the head of Le Garzac until his parachute snagged on a tree and he was suspended 10 feet above ground.

'Shit,' said a voice with a French accent. 'I've lost my glasses. Bloody hell, I can't see anything!'

Hibbert emerged out of the darkness, laughing, and hailed the dangling man as he stood directly below him, as 'Mickey'. 'Mickey' was Lieutenant Michele Pinci, the 21-year-old son of Count Mario Pinci, of French-Italian extraction, and his Australian wife, Gwen. Pinci told Hibbert not to worry, he had a second pair of glasses.

There were other additions, too, in the SAS camp over the course of their stay: five airmen, including two Americans, who had baled out of their stricken aircraft in the preceding weeks and spent the interim sheltering with the Maquis.

On 21 August the SAS scored their first significant success when they ambushed a German column on the road from Langres to Châteauvillain. Two jeeps, one commanded by Lieutenant Morris and the other by Sergeant Charles Linton, had been in position since before dawn, watching and waiting for the right moment. They allowed six empty Nazi trucks to pass, then an armoured car and a truck full of troops. At 1300 hours the British heard the sound of more engines. This time it was two trucks laden with troops, the vehicles about 400 yards apart. Morris gave the nod to Linton. 'Sgt. Linton, who was nearest, engaged the first vehicle with all three Vickers and one Bren,' ran the report on the ambush. 'The German troops crowded on top of this vehicle were swept off by the fire and provided, as Lieut. Morris describes, a truly remarkable sight. The vehicle came to a halt opposite this second jeep, which opened up and completely shattered it.'

The second truck, meanwhile, had pulled off the road and startled Nazis were hastily disembarking, seeking cover in the verge and the foliage that bordered the country road. One German, on top of the cab, opened up with an MG42 but was promptly silenced by a burst of fire from James Downey. The Germans who had sought refuge soon began 'returning an accurate fire' so Morris ordered the two jeeps to withdraw. It had been a profitable day's hunting: an estimate of thirty enemy dead and no SAS casualties.

The next day Hibbert and a section of men shot up a German truck and the day after, 23 August, Morris and Robertson led a patrol into the village of Giey-sur-Aujon en route to sabotage the main railway line between Langres and Dijon. Villagers immediately cautioned that close at hand were some Nazi soldiers, specifically White Russians, so-called because they were the descendants of the White Army, the name given to the Russian soldiers who had fought for the Czar against the Bolshevik army during the Revolution a quarter of a century earlier. The SAS dismounted and headed into Giey-sur-Aujon on foot. 'Firing opened at once and an occasional startled Russian could be seen starting off down the street,' wrote Morris in his report. Robertson shot one dead with his 'first shot': not just his first shot with the SAS but the first bullet he had fired in anger in the war. On reaching the village churchyard, Morris peered over the wall and was 'alarmed to discover Russian soldiers doing the same 5 yards to his right'. Morris was first on the draw, hurling a grenade into the churchyard. 'There was a stampede and frantic shouting among the Russians,' he recalled. Morris and his corporal, Harris, anticipated the direction in which their enemy would run and met them with machine-gun fire. 'The Russians turned round and ran faster than before.' The Russians offered no further resistance and the SAS continued on their way, successfully blowing the railway line and returning to base without incident.

On 24 August Captain Hibbert lunched with a leader of a local Resistance Group, and discovered to his delight that a fellow guest was Lieutenant Jim Mackie, who had recently arrived in the area with the rest of C Squadron as part of Operation Wallace.

Five days earlier the squadron had emplaned at Brize Norton in twenty Dakotas, a total of sixty soldiers and twenty jeeps. They touched down at Rennes aerodrome at 1630 hours on 19 August, minus two aircraft that were forced to return to England. The following morning the convoy of eighteen jeeps began the 375-mile drive east towards the Plateau de Langres, rendez-vousing briefly at Le Mans with Lieutenant Colonel Blair Mayne, CO of 1SAS, who had arrived in France a fortnight earlier. He offered to provide a guide for Farran as far as the city of Orleans, north of which was a 1SAS Operation codenamed 'Gain'. But a guide could not be found so 2SAS moved off alone and reached Orleans in the evening of 20 August. The American 45th Armored Division provided the British with petrol and rations, and Farran and his men were in good heart as they continued their journey east the following morning. Many of the men in the convoy had crossed southern Italy in similar fashion in September 1943 and they were familiar with Farran's system for crossing a main road: a point was selected where a track

Some of the men who participated in Operation Wallace.

Roy Farran was a brilliant special forces soldier, possessing initiative, guile and aggression.

or a minor road traversed the main road, ideally under cover. A forward patrol would indicate when the road was clear and the squadron then drove across at high speed in close column.

The greater part of 22 August was given over to intelligence gathering and Captain Lee proved 'invaluable' in extracting information from villagers as to the disposition of German troops. Lee was a *nom de guerre*; his real name was Raymond Couraud, a 24-year-old from western France with an American mother, who in 1938 had enlisted in the French Foreign Legion posing as a Belgian. Decorated for gallantry during the Norwegian Campaign in 1940, Lee took part in the battle for France and subsequently fled Vichy France for the Mediterranean city of Marseille. For a while he became involved in the flourishing black market, smuggling in goods to the port and selling them on. At some point he made the acquaintance of an American socialite called Mary Jayne Gold, and they became lovers. Gold had lived in Paris for a number of years but she travelled south to escape the Nazis with the intention of catching a ship back to the States. Instead she became involved in the Emergency Rescue Committee [ERC], an organization run by American Varian Fry, using her money to help finance the evacuation from France to neutral Spain or the USA of an estimated 2,000 European refugees, many of them Jews. Lee was not appreciated by Fry and the other members of the ERC, who regarded him as a hoodlum and a bad influence on Gold. Their solution in April 1941 was to smuggle Lee to Spain, from where he travelled to England, serving first with SOE and then with the commandos. He was the only Frenchman to participate in the St Nazaire raid in March 1942, where he was wounded in the legs, and upon his recovery he was posted to No. 62 Commando, under the command of Lieutenant Colonel Bill Stirling. When this unit evolved into 2SAS in May 1943, Lee commanded a small group of Frenchmen who were attached to the regiment and participated in several operations in Italy in the summer and autumn of that year. Farran considered him a brilliant guerrilla soldier and admitted that in 1943 he 'learnt a lot' from the Frenchman. When Lee arrived in France with 2SAS he had probably heard that his father had died at Buchenwald in January 1944. He was therefore out to kill as many Germans as possible.

On the evening of 22 August Farran split his force in three: a section of eight jeeps under his command and two sections of five vehicles under Lee and Lieutenant David Leigh, a newly married officer who possessed 'considerable experience of operations of this nature'. The three columns set off at intervals of 30 minutes on the same route with instructions to avoid the enemy to the best of their ability. Alas, reflected Farran, 'the Latin temperament is a most incalculable factor', and Lee decided to 'charge through the first opposition he encountered on the east side of the River Yonne', just after the village of Mailly-le-Château. The villagers had warned Lee of the enemy dug in on the river bank but he forced a passage through, although German fire hit the fourth jeep in the convoy, immobilising the vehicle without wounding any of the three occupants.

The three columns rendezvoused in the forest of St Jean, 100 miles behind the front, and an irate Farran reduced Lee's convoy to two jeeps as a punishment for his disobedience. Shortly before dusk on 23 August they continued their journey east. Lee's two jeeps departed first at 1700 hours and Leigh's column of six jeeps was last to leave at 1845 hours. The direction was southeast towards the village of Bierry-les-Belles-Fontaines and then on through Villaines-les-Prévôtes.

Lee was more prudent than on the previous night and approached each village cautiously. A local assured him that Villaines-les-Prévôtes was free of Germans so his vehicle, followed by that of Lieutenant Lord John Manners, the 22-year-old son of the Marquess of Granby, drove into the village. The road ascended and curved to the right at the village church. Lee saw someone on the road. A German. He squeezed the trigger of the Vickers and the German fell onto the road. The local who had told Lee the coast was clear hadn't known that earlier that day a company of Germans had laagered in Villaines-les-Prévôtes.

More of the enemy appeared. Lee gave them another burst and his driver, Private Len Rudd, known as Pirate Bill, swung the jeep left and accelerated up the Place de la Fontaine. Manners' vehicle followed. But it was a cul-de-sac. The lead vehicle crashed into the wall at the end of the cul-de-sac. Rudd's head bounced off the steering wheel, and he probably lost consciousness for a few moments. Lieutenant Ralph Dodds was also injured and was helped out of the vehicle by Lance Corporal Stanley Walsh. Lee, Manners and two soldiers called Rushbrook and O'Callaghan jumped over a fence and ran into

Lieutenant Lord John Manners (*right*), pictured before Operation Wallace.

the fields that sloped upwards towards the village cemetery. Walsh helped the limping Dodds over the fence and then turned to give his comrades time to escape. The Germans were Afrika Korps, not long back from Italy, some still wearing their khaki shorts and blue shirts. They advanced cautiously up the cul-de-sac. Walsh rose from behind a jeep and levelled his Thompson sub-machine gun at the enemy. To his horror his gun jammed, 'whereupon he rushed at two of the enemy who were approaching, knocking both down with his weapon. In spite of the fact he was wounded by a grenade, Walsh then killed or wounded two more of the enemy, after which he was finally taken prisoner.'

As for Len Rudd, according to a subsequent statement given to Captain Christopher Sykes, the 2SAS intelligence officer, by the Mayor of Villaines-les-Prévôtes, Monsieur Vaillard, the Englishman 'mounted a staircase and was killed in falling'.

A few minutes later Major Farran's convoy approached Villaines-les-Prévôtes, by which time the Germans had positioned a 75mm field gun just round the bend at the entrance to the village. Farran screamed to his driver, Corporal Clarke, to swing into the ditch on the left of the road. At the same moment the gun fired. 'Perhaps it was because we were so close to the muzzle of the gun that the shell whistled over our heads to burst in the road behind,' remarked Farran.

The last of the eight jeeps in Farran's column was under the command of Sergeant Harry Vickers. 'Everything was so peaceful,' recalled Vickers. 'My driver was Harry Cockerill, I was in the front passenger seat and in the back was Bill Holland, who had come from the London Irish. He was a good lad. We heard this explosion, completed the turn of the bend and Farran was out of his jeep getting everyone organised. Farran said 'Get on the flank with the Bren gun,' so I went with Holland down this hedge and, though I tell the tale against myself, I was most interested in the leaves that were coming off the tree above my head. It was bullets cutting the leaves off. This was my first time in a fire-fight.'

Farran had ordered Corporal Clarke and Lieutenant Brian 'Chips' Carpendale, his wireless operator, to site a Bren gun on top of the bank that over-looked the left of the road. He then moved back down his column shouting precise instructions. Vickers and Holland were told to cover the right flank, along with Lieutenant Jim Mackie's jeep, which included Joe Cunningham. 'He was a great character,' remembered Vickers. 'The stones were bouncing up by his boots from the German bullets and I said to him "Joe, what's that round your feet?" "Grasshoppers", he said. He was a dry stick, was Joe.'

In his report of the incident at Villaines-les-Prévôtes Farran said that at one moment the Germans called on him to surrender. His response was a burst from his carbine. The Germans' reply was a salvo of mortar rounds and some shells from the 75mm. Then the Afrika Korps 'made a charge along both sides of the road and the SAS had a magnificent shoot at less than 50 yards range'.

Vickers held his fire until the last moment, watching the Germans in their khaki shorts and blue shirts. 'When they lined up and charged us they were shouting "English Schweinhund" and I remember thinking at the time "They always used to shout that in the Boys' Own books I read about the First War and they are actually shouting it!". Holland and I were behind this hedge and they all lined up on the other side of the hedge and moved down. We just sprayed them as they charged.'

The Germans retreated and for several minutes the two sides exchanged desultory fire. The battle of Villaines-les-Prévôtes had been raging for nearly an hour, and Farran wondered where David Leigh's column had got to. Suddenly 'a mortar and a machine gun opened up in the rear of the SAS party'. It was Farran's cue to withdraw before they were encircled, and they pulled out down a lane that led to a mill. There the track stopped so Farran led them across country until they debouched onto a country lane near Jeux. From there they continued their drive towards the forest base of Operation Hardy.

Whatever had delayed Lieutenant Leigh's column, it proved fatal. When they arrived at Villaines-les-Prévôtes Farran had departed but the Germans had not. 'We hadn't heard anything,' recalled Lieutenant Alex Robertson. This was probably on account of what another soldier in the column, Lance Corporal Harold 'Tanky' Challenor, described as a 'tremendous thunderstorm'. Like a number of 2SAS veterans from North Africa, Challenor had contracted recurrent malaria and the illness usually flared up when he got soaked. He therefore uncorked a bottle of local plum wine and, for medicinal purposes, took a couple of generous swigs. Challenor was in the third jeep and Robertson in the rear as they neared the village. 'I was at the back of the column and the first I knew was turning a corner to see David Leigh lying wounded in his jeep and Ron McEachan [a signaller] dead on the ground,' recalled Robertson.

Assuming command, Hugh Gurney shouted orders with cool alacrity and the remaining jeeps reversed down the road and made good their escape. According to Challenor, he couldn't reverse his vehicle because of the trailer he was towing, so he and the two men in the jeep dashed up the bank and hid in the bushes on the outskirts of Villaines-les-Prévôtes. They remained there the whole night, emerging at dawn to discover that the Afrika Korps had pulled out in the hours of darkness. Challenor's jeep was where he had left it, and they set off on the tail of their comrades.

Although Gurney had lost three men in the skirmish, on withdrawing from Villaines-les-Prévôtes he had picked up Captain Lee and his party. With their four jeeps already overcrowded, it was decided to leave the body of McEachan, a 25-year-old married man from Edinburgh, at the same mill that

Hugh Gurney was an aggressive officer who thrived under Farran's command.

Farran's convoy had passed. The column raced 9 miles south-west to Époisses with Leigh still clinging to life. 'David had been hit in the chest,' remembered Robertson. 'I drove to Époisses and knocked on the door of a cheesemaker called Pierre Berthaut. He helped me carry David upstairs to the bedroom while his wife went to fetch a doctor.' She returned with a doctor no more than ten minutes later, but it was too late. Leigh was dead.

Leaving Leigh's body in Époisses, Lee's column set off with the intention of reaching the 1SAS base in Avallon. But their bearings were out, and instead of driving west they went north. On approaching the village of Bierry-les-Belles-Fontaines around midnight they were challenged in the dark by a German sentry stationed in a farmyard. His bullet grazed the head of Lieutenant Edmund Birtwistle, a 20-year-old officer on his first operation. His good fortune was monumental. The bullet rendered him unconscious but there was no significant wound.

Of greater concern to the SAS was how to extricate themselves from Bierry-les-Belles-Fontaines. The streets were narrow and Lee gave the order to dismount and withdraw on foot. Sergeant Pete Tomasso, an Italian-born Scot who had distinguished himself with the regiment in Italy the previous year, 'retained his presence of mind and backed his jeep, which was the last in the column, up the hill'. Most of the other men scattered across fields and took refuge under hedgerows. When it became apparent that there was only a small detachment of Germans in the village, four SAS soldiers returned to collect the jeeps. Eventually Lee's column reached Avallon, from where they were flown back to England. Both Brian Franks and Roy Farran were furious with Lee for not rejoining the rest of Wallace. In a radio signal the latter described him as 'a bastard', a rare display of emotion in the normally terse exchange of communications. Franks had him placed under close arrest for dereliction of duty.

Farran and his seven jeeps, meanwhile, driving at a steady 5mph, were approaching the southern extremity of the forest of Châtillon-sur-Seine on the morning of 24 August when a goods train was heard coming down the line. 'It was engaged with mixed incendiaries, tracer and A.P. [Armour Piercing] from all the Vickers at 15 yards range, and stopped in a cloud of steam and smoke,' Farran commented in his report. Hissing and belching, the train rolled on for 200 yards and then came to a halt. The driver alighted from his cab and, surveying the wreck, shrugged his shoulders.

Lying up in the forest of Châtillon-sur-Seine, Farran despatched Jim Mackie to find Grant Hibbert, which he did at a lunch date with the Maquis. Operations Wallace and Hardy united at 1500 hours at the latter's forest hideout, 'in thick undergrowth so that the tents [made from parachute silks] would be invisible from the air'. Between them they had ten jeeps, a civilian car, a beat-up 10-ton truck that was used to ferry resupplies dropped by the RAF to their base, and sixty soldiers.

Edmund Birtwistle had a lucky escape when a bullet grazed his head at Bierry-les-Belles.

Hibbert briefed Farran on the lie of the land, the effectiveness of the Maquis, the reliability of the locals and the movements of the enemy. The following evening Farran was treated to a resupply, and he was also introduced by Hibbert to the leader of the main Maquis group at Aigny-le-Duc, approximately 15 miles south of the SAS base, a man called Colonel Claude. John Wiseman, of A Squadron, 1SAS, was also present, and the British officers and their French brothers-in-arms enjoyed several glasses of vermouth while toasting the King and General de Gaulle.

On 27 August the combined squadron began offensive patrols on the roads leading west to Châtillon-sur-Seine. Lieutenant Pinci and Sergeant Linton destroyed a petrol wagon, killing seven Germans. That night there was a resupply, which included two reinforcements, one of whom was a popular

Tim Robinson was a 2SAS veteran who served under Farran in Italy and on Wallace.

soldier called Joachim Kalkstein, a 'happy lad', according to Harry Vickers. Nicknamed 'Joe', Kalkstein had been born in Berlin in 1920 to Polish Jews who ran a shoe shop. Like so many other German Jews, Joe fled the country once the Nazis came to power and fought as a teenager with the International Brigade in the Spanish Civil War. He also served in the Palestine Police and joined 2SAS in 1943 when they were stationed in North Africa.

Kalkstein had come through many adventures in his young life but on this night his good fortune expired. 'Kalkstein dropped and his 'chute didn't open,' recalled Vickers. 'We heard him go through the trees. He never shouted or made a noise. Funny that.' It was surmised that his static line had been corroded by acid. The next day Kalkstein was laid to rest in the village cemetery at Recey-sur-Ource. In a letter to Kalkstein's cousin, Captain Hibbert described the scene: 'He was buried next day, after a full church service at which some 500 people attended, in the cemetery at Recey-sur-Ource along with seven RAF personnel who had crashed there some time previously. He will be a great loss to the squadron and the Regiment. He was very popular amongst the men and deservedly looked on as an extremely good, efficient and cheerful soldier by all the officers.'

The squadron scored several notable successes on 28 August and the following day, emboldened, Farran led a patrol towards Châtillon-sur-Seine, approaching from the east. Their intelligence was that a German HQ had been established in a farm at La Barotte, a couple of miles east of the town, but a member of the Maquis telephoned the mayor of Châtillon and he confirmed that the Nazis had set up a new HQ in the Château Marmont, to the west of the town. Described by Farran as being situated 'on a high hill', the château was experiencing its third war. Partially destroyed by the Prussians during the war of 1870, it had served as Maréchal Joseph Joffre's headquarters from the outbreak of the First World War in August 1914 to the end of September that year during the Battle of the Marne. Farran and his men approached the château on foot from the east 'to inspect the German trucks'. There were twenty in total and, according to the mayor, approximately 150 Germans inside the château and its buildings.

That evening, 29 August, Farran and Hibbert dined with Colonel Claude and 'it was decided to make a joint attack on Châtillon the following day'. Claude promised to furnish 500 armed Maquis as long as they were given enough petrol for their fleet of trucks. In his report on Operation Wallace, Farran wrote of what came to be called the Battle of Châtillon: 'The plan was to seize the important road junction and crossroads with jeeps and then to send a foot party, with Brens carried by jeeps, as far as possible to the back of the château. The signal for the attack to begin was to be when the 3" mortar opened fire on the château.'

The attack began at first light. Lieutenant Jim Mackie and ten jeeps took up position on the Montbard-Châtillon-Dijon crossroads to the south of the town,

The grave of 'Joe' Kalkstein in Recey-sur-Ource.

while the rest of the squadron – forty-four men in nine jeeps – headed into the centre of Châtillon-sur-Seine. 'Lieut Mackie placed his jeep in the middle of the crossroads and sent Sgt Vickers' jeep down the road leading to Montbard, as that seemed the most likely line of enemy approach,' wrote Farran.

By 0700 hours the whole squadron was in place on other approaches into the town and the telephone wires had been cut. The first of forty-eight mortar bombs landed on Château Marmont on the hour. Fifteen minutes later, wrote Farran, a column of German reinforcements, consisting of thirty trucks, arrived at the river bridge: 'Sgt Vickers allowed them to close to 20 yards' range.'

Vickers had in fact expected to welcome the 500 armed Maquis, and Lieutenant Mackie had cautioned him not to open fire on them by mistake. 'This convoy appeared and I wondered if it was the French because there were no markings on the trucks,' recalled Vickers. 'I waited until the very end and it was only when I saw their big hats that I realised they were Germans. We had me and the twin Vickers, Harry Cockerill, the driver with a carbine and on the other side of the road behind the telegraph pole was [Bill] Holland with a Bren.' Farran had also attached one of Lieutenant Morris's mortar section men to Vickers, who had with him a 2-inch mortar.

Farran described in his report that the first five trucks, two of which were loaded with ammunition, 'were brewed up and caused a great firework display'. A motorcycle combination was also destroyed. 'It was all a bit

This is the approximate position of Harry Vickers when he engaged the Germans as they drove north-east across the bridge.

The view looking south-west from the roundabout where Jim Mackie was positioned. The bridge is around 300 metres down the road.

bloody really,' reflected Vickers. 'When we started firing we didn't have any cover, we were in the middle of the road. I remember there was a bay over the piers of the masonry bridge, it was a little platform where the pavement bulged out and if you got down behind there you were all right and protected. One or two of the lads were behind these refilling the magazines.'

Vickers recalled that they 'received a lot of incoming fire from the Germans' and one round hit Bill Holland. By now the rest of Mackie's section had joined the fray and one soldier, Private Charlie Hackney, recalled: 'There were bullets flying all over the place and we shot around half a dozen Germans as we battled our way up the street. Then we saw a man in the doorway signalling to us and we found Bill Holland dying on the floor of his house. Jim Mackie leant over him but there was nothing we could do.' The house was No. 4 avenue Joffre, 20 metres from the Montbard-Châtillon-Dijon crossroad, occupied by Monsieur and Madame Bienaime.

To the north-west, some of the 150-strong German garrison from Château Marmont were endeavouring to reinforce their comrades. They advanced south along the Rue Marmont but ran into an SAS section deployed on the roundabout at Place Marmont. 'Fierce street fighting developed and the Germans succeeded in mortaring some of their own men,' wrote Farran. At 0830 hours Farran instructed Morris's mortar section to support their comrades at the Place Marmont. Nevertheless, at 0845 hours the SAS were 'subjected to such strong pressure on the crossroads from Germans in the houses

Destruction in Châtillon-sur-Seine.

Charlie Hackney, a Chelsea
Pensioner in the 2000s, was
a 2SAS veteran who
parachuted into Wallace
with Mike Pinci.

that, although only one jeep had been damaged and one man killed [Holland], Major Farran felt that the absence of the promised Maquis made his position untenable, particularly as the tail of the enemy column on the Montbard road was by now more organised'. Farran fired two Verey lights, the signal for a squadron withdrawal.

Elements of the Maquis were encountered as the SAS commenced their withdrawal but, noted Farran, they did not 'appear inclined to give full scale support'. Skirmishes continued for the rest of the morning but the SAS returned to their base having suffered one fatality and two wounded. The two jeeps that had been damaged were soon repaired. 'A conservative estimate of the enemy casualties is at least 100 Germans killed and a considerable number wounded,' wrote Farran. 'Nine trucks, two cars and one motor-cycle were destroyed.'

Reports later reached the SAS that the Germans rounded up fifty locals with the intention of executing them 'for what they had imagined was a Maquis raid'. When they found the body of Bill Holland they released their hostages and set out to hunt down the British commandos.

On the night of 30/31 August there was a much-needed resupply drop of two jeeps and fifty-two containers, crammed with ammunition, rations and clothing. The next night four more jeeps and five reinforcements arrived by parachute, one of whom was Lieutenant Bob Walker-Brown. Formerly of the Highland Light Infantry, Walker-Brown had fought in some of the fiercest engagements in North Africa before he was captured in the 'Battle of the Cauldron' in June 1942. He had spent fifteen months as a POW in Italy before escaping and returning to Britain where he volunteered for the SAS. 'Farran was a born soldier; he had drive and initiative and was quite ruthless,' Walker-Brown said of Farran. 'If someone didn't measure up, he was out.'

Farran now split his force into three:

(1) Nine jeeps with twenty-six all ranks, under his command, to operate immediately from a base in the Forest of Drancy, 80 miles north-east of Châtillon and 25 miles south-west of Épinal.

(2) Nine jeeps of twenty-nine all ranks, commanded by Captain Hibbert, to move east three days after Farran's departure to the area north of Bourbonne-les-Bains.

(3) Twenty-three all ranks operating on foot under Lieutenant Pinci in the Plateau de Langres, targeting enemy vehicles on the roads from Châtillon to Chaumont, Chaumont to Langres and Langres to Dijon.

Farran's journey east was for the most part uneventful, save for the odd encounter with stray enemy vehicles that were clinically despatched. The greatest impediment to his passage to the Forest of Drancy was 'the enthusiasm of the locals, who heralded his arrival [in each village] with the ringing of church bells, militarily inconvenient'. They arrived at their destination of the

Lieutenant Walker-Brown (*far right*), seen here with his troop prior to operations in Italy in December 1944, was an able and admired officer.

evening of 4 September, and the next day patrols began reconnoitring the vicinity. Lieutenant Mackie surprised a German motorcycle combination carrying seven soldiers, and only one escaped.

On the night of 6/7 September Farran welcomed three familiar faces into his camp: Lieutenant Hugh Gurney, Lance Corporal Tanky Challenor and Private Bob Fyfe. The trio had been members of David Leigh's patrol at the battle of Villaines-les-Prévôtes, and subsequently were evacuated to England by air. Unfortunately, Farran wrote in his report, they 'were attacked on the DZ, in the morning, by 600 SS troops with four armoured cars, six troop carriers and twenty staff cars'. The Maquis had raised the alarm at 0630 hours and there was but a small window of opportunity for the SAS to escape. Rousing the six jeep crews, they moved their vehicles out of the woods on the field that a few hours earlier had served as a DZ. By now the Germans had been engaged by the Maquis on the eastern side of the wood. Their routes to the north and west were blocked by a deep stream that flowed across the field and for a moment Farran contemplated circling the jeeps and, like General Custer at the battle of the Little Big Horn, fighting it out to the last man. Then he spotted a gap in the south-west corner of the field, 'through which the jeeps crashed', emerging onto a track that led to the main road.

Farran ordered Lieutenant Gurney to take two jeeps and attack the enemy's rear along the Grandrupt Road while Sergeant Vickers was instructed to establish an ambush position a mile to their east, by the village of Hennezel, in the expectation that the Nazis would withdraw in that direction.

With Gurney was Tanky Challenor, who recalled that they soon spotted a group of SS officers standing on a small rise directing operations. 'Mr Gurney immediately opened fire with the front pair of Vickers and I joined in with the single,' said Challenor. 'We accounted for them all and brewed up their HQ truck for good measure.'

Vickers remembered: 'Farran pulled up and said to me "Stay here, Vickers, and see if you can hold them up." Then off he went and left us there. I'm not complaining about that. We suddenly heard these two fast cars approaching, outside Hennezel that was, and I got the colonel and his 2 i/c, although I didn't know that at the time.' In fact, the two German officers shot dead by Vickers were on their way to direct the SS attack.

For the next few days the SAS remained constantly on the move, eluding the vengeful Nazis on their trail. Farran was delighted to see the return of Lieutenant Carpendale, who during a three-day patrol had attacked a German billet and killed twenty men as they carried out their ablutions in a farmyard. However, he also brought unwelcome news from Epinal, which had been reinforced by the arrival of around 2,000 troops as the Germans sought to beef up the defences on the Moselle Line. 'The chances were that General Patton was about to receive a check,' commented Farran.

Lieutenant Gurney was particularly aggressive in his pursuit of the enemy, which Challenor attributed to a desire to avenge his retreat from Villaines the previous month. On 11 September Gurney intercepted and destroyed a staff car, killing several officers, one of whom, the Maquis subsequently informed the SAS, was a general.

The next day Gurney and two jeeps approached Velorcey, entering from the north along a forest track that joined a paved road through the small village. They continued a few hundred yards south along the road to the edge of the village where it formed a t-junction with the main road to Meurcourt to the west. Gurney positioned his jeeps on either side of the t-junction. 'It was almost dark and quiet,' remembered Challenor. 'You could hear the humming of the insects and the last calls of the birds. Waiting. The time of tension.'

Gurney passed the time by explaining to Challenor the variety of grapes used in the production of wine. Challenor listened attentively, in awe of 'an officer and a gentleman' who because of his consideration and kindness had 'become almost a father figure in my life, as I had known a drunken brute as a father'.

Suddenly, above the songs of the birds, the SAS heard another sound. It came from the east, and was approaching along the main road. 'We strained our eyes and I saw a monstrous lorry in the lead,' said Challenor. Gurney instructed his men to hold their fire until his command. There were other vehicles in the column but the fire from the jeep's machine guns was directed at the head of the convoy when it was 10 yards distant. 'An intensive hail of tracer and incendiary raked the cab and sides,' recalled Challenor. 'Then it happened. With a tremendous roar and yellow glare it blew up.'

The lorry was full of explosives and it detonated with such force that the SAS soldiers were flattened by the shockwaves. Challenor rose unsteadily to his feet, blood streaming from a wound to his eye. 'Get out of it,' yelled Gurney. Challenor tried to start the jeep but to no avail. Gurney ordered Challenor and Fyfe to make for the second jeep that was doing a U-turn ready to roar north through the village. Challenor, still in a daze, staggered across the t-junction. His officer urged him on. 'The Germans were coming down the lane firing automatic weapons,' said Challenor. Gurney was hit in the back and fell to the road dead. Fyfe ran back and pulled Challenor on board the jeep. 'As we thrashed madly up the track I fell unconscious off the jeep but they came back and slung me on again,' said Challenor.

The SAS reported Gurney's death in a signal sent to England on 13 September: 'Gurney killed,' it ran. 'Germans refused to allow the burial of "American terrorists" but civilians buried [him] today.'

On 11 September, the day before Gurney's death, Hibbert's party had also suffered a tragedy while operating in the area north of Bourbonne-les-Bains, where their most notable success was the destruction of a huge petrol dump.

Private James Downey, who had demonstrated his mettle on several occasions during Operation Hardy, was leaning against his jeep as Corporal Clarke inspected the twin Vickers in the rear of the vehicle. Clarke removed one of the drum magazines and a round was discharged. It hit Downey in the stomach, and 'sprayed out inside him, destroying his intestines and left lung'. It took the popular Lancastrian an hour to die, a traumatic experience for all his comrades who witnessed the incident. The next day he was buried in the village cemetery of Varennes-sur-Amance. An examination of the Vickers concluded that the gun 'could not have been completely cocked and must have been resting on the base of the next round'.

The third of the three Wallace/Hardy parties, that commanded by Lieutenant Mike Pinci, had been operating on the Plateau de Langres since 1 September on what officially was termed Operation Robey. For three days Pinci disappeared on what he called an 'extensive recce', one that entailed visiting his family in Paris in a commandeered car. In his absence Lieutenant Bob Walker-Brown, who had obtained three vehicles from the Maquis, ambushed a German column on 8 September, acting on information from the French that four or five petrol bowsers would be travelling south towards Chatillon-sur-Seine at first light. 'We took the advice of the French and chose the position at a point where the country road crossed the main road,' recalled Walker-Brown. 'We allowed the German leading escort vehicles to run

The site of Walker-Brown's ambush, from the bank where the SAS were positioned, looking towards the road down which the Germans drove, from right to left, in the direction of the signpost marked 'Auxerre'.

through the killing area, thinking they would continue south. As we opened up on the fuel bowsers, which did go up in quite a cloud of smoke, we were suddenly fired on.' The German escort had swung round and attacked the SAS from the rear. 'We had a very unpleasant job extricating ourselves,' recalled Walker-Brown, but they did so without sustaining any casualties.

Pinci returned to the SAS base at Auberive on the morning of Sunday, 11 September and was soon off again, this time to Recey-sur-Ource for a celebratory lunch with the Maquis in the town hall. Jean Le Garzic recalled that they toasted the recent liberation of Paris and when Pinci left in the early afternoon he was sent on his way with a resounding cheer from all present. He climbed into his civilian car and set off behind an SAS jeep containing three soldiers. But he had overlooked one crucial detail: the white star on the roof or bonnet that was a recognition sign for all marauding Allied aircraft. The jeep had a star on its bonnet, but Pinci's vehicle didn't.

'I was myself in the vehicle he was driving, in which there was also Colonel Michel, commanding FFI in the department of Haute Marne,' said a Maquisard called Pouztale in a written statement five days later.

Just over a mile east of Recey, on the road towards Langres, by the left turn to Gurgy-le-Château, the cars were spotted by two Allied fighter aircraft, presumed to be American P-47 Thunderbolts. 'Two bursts of shells straddled the vehicles,' remembered Poutzale. 'We thought at first that we were under machine-gun fire from an ambush. As Lieut. Pinci braked to prepare to fight, a third burst struck his car, covering it with hits. He himself was struck in the head and killed on the spot.'

According to Sergeant Jim Chambers, a member of the Jedburgh 'Bunny' team operating in the area, Pinci had asked him to radio a message to SAS HQ in England asking for an air strike on a large concentration of Germans withdrawing towards the Belfort Gap to their east. 'I did this, I transmitted the message and got confirmation that an air strike would take place,' recalled Chambers. Pinci then decided 'that he would go with the Maquis to have a look at this air strike, and they went off in two cars and unfortunately only one had the Allied white star on the roof. These cars were travelling together and the aircraft came over to do the strike and it was believed that the pilot of one thought it was a German car chasing a Maquis car … and he strafed the car.'

Two days later Walker-Brown attacked the village of Saints-Geosmes, just south of Langres, on what he called a 'mortar shoot'. From a distance of 800 yards they opened fire on the German garrison with a 3-inch mortar sited in the back of a car. 'It had a sliding roof and we whittled away the roof and enlarged it, stuffed the mortar inside, having taken the back seat out, on top of a lot of sandbags,' explained Walker-Brown. 'We were extremely nervous because when a bomb was put down the spout the car bottomed and God knows where it went. It landed somewhere, we didn't give a bugger where it landed, as long as it landed, but it was slightly nerve-wracking being in the car because if the bomb had hit the roof it would have been unpleasant. We fired groups of three rounds rapid, so probably about nine bombs. Having done the attack we were fired on but they were firing blind and hadn't located us.'

It was, said Walker-Brown, 'a flea bite' of an attack but one nonetheless that increased the insecurity of the Nazis, who found themselves in the middle of a guerrilla army that was inflicting casualties almost on a daily basis. But a day later, 14 September, Operation Hardy/Wallace reached the end of its shelf life with the arrival of the vanguard of General Philippe Leclerc's 2nd Armored Division. 'So we introduced ourselves and assisted in the capture of Langres,' recalled Walker-Brown.

The SAS Brigade described Hardy/Wallace as 'the most successful [operation] of any hitherto undertaken in France by the 2nd SAS Regiment, largely because the timing happened to be opportune'. That was obviously critical. Unstated by the brigade, but tacitly acknowledged and just as important, was the fact that most of C Squadron were experienced members of the SAS who had seen action in Italy the previous year. In soldiers' jargon, they liked a scrap and knew how to handle themselves. This wasn't the case with some other 2SAS operations (and also 1SAS operations, such as Bulbasket, which ended in tragedy) which involved new recruits to the regiment. These men were brave, willing and enthusiastic, but inexperienced in guerrilla warfare. Farran and Hibbert, on the other hand, had under their command numerous men who could cope physically and psychologically with the pressure of operating deep behind enemy lines – soldiers such as Tomasso, Challenor, Holland, Lee, Hackney and Jim Mackie. The only weak link had been a few junior officers who didn't lack for courage but nonetheless were dangerously callow. 'Lack of previous training made it necessary for the jeeps to move from one area to another in large parties under experienced officers,' wrote Farran in his report. 'If sufficient troop leaders of high quality, reliability and experience had been available, I believe that more damage could have been inflicted on the enemy by widely dispersed troops, only regrouping periodically for resupply ... I suggest that no officers who have not had previous active service experience in a service unit should be recruited. Extremely young officers are usually an embarrassment in operations of this nature.'

The official statistics for Hardy/Wallace were a testament to their relentlessness: 500 enemy soldiers killed or wounded, twenty-three staff cars destroyed, along with six motorcycles and thirty-six 'miscellaneous vehicles', including trucks, an ammunition truck and several petrol bowsers. A petrol dump believed to have contained 100,000 gallons was set ablaze and a goods train was shot up. All told, 116 soldiers had participated in Hardy/Wallace.

Eight of them had lost their lives, another seven had been wounded and two, Lieutenant Ralph Dodds and Lance Corporal Stan Walsh, had been captured.

In his report Farran outlined why their marauding patrols had been so effective. 'In ambuscades, it is better to sacrifice cover to enable the jeep to take on targets at close range,' he wrote. 'The Twin-Vickers Gun will cut a truck in half at under 50 yards, but at greater range is too inaccurate. The principles of a good ambush are as follows:

1. A position where the jeep cannot be seen until the target is within range, but where the jeep is certain of getting a long burst into the bonnet of the truck as soon as it appears. A burst in the front part of a vehicle will set it on fire nine times out of ten.
2. A good covered withdrawal.
3. No banks or undergrowth which enemy troops can use for retaliatory fire.
4. As soon as sufficient damage has been done the jeep must disappear. It is not necessary to stay long enough to count the bodies.'

Visiting the operational area of Hardy/Wallace

Hardy DZ

Strictly speaking, Operation Hardy/Wallace began in the Morvan where, on the night of 26/27 July, the advance party arrived by parachute to be met by A Squadron, 1SAS, members of Operation Houndsworth, but here we shall begin retracing its movements 65 miles to the north-east. Operation Houndsworth is covered in the first volume of the SAS in France, and the DZ on which Hardy/Wallace landed can be located in a clearing deep in the forest of Montsauche, a short signposted walk from the Maquis cemetery (**GPS 47.185930, 4.002345**).

Once Grant Hibbert had established a base for Hardy, the next task was to organise a resupply and the site chosen was at La Maison-Neuve, a couple of miles north of the village of Recey-sur-Ource, known to the Maquis by its codename 'Bronchite' (**GPS 47.810415, 4.844945**).

It was here that Joachim 'Joe' Kalkstein met his end on the night of 27/28 August when his parachute failed to open. He was buried the next day in the village cemetery at Recey-sur-Ource (**GPS 47.782315, 4.856056**) in a ceremony attended by hundreds of locals. In 1996 Freddie Oakes, a veteran of 2SAS, visited the cemetery with his son William to pay his respects to Kalkstein. Noticing that the gravestone did not bear the Star of David as was the custom with Jewish soldiers, William contacted the Commonwealth War Graves Commission (CWGC) in the hope of rectifying this oversight. They explained that only a relative could make such a demand so William embarked on a mission to locate some of Kalkstein's flesh and blood. Eventually he traced his elder sister, Ursel Levy, and she wrote to the CWGC with a request that the Star of David be added to the headstone, along with the inscription:

IN MEMORY OF OUR BROTHER
BORN IN BERLIN
21ST JULY 1920
URSEL AND NORBERT

Norbet was Joachim's twin brother. Ursel died not long after the inscription was added.

Kalstein's gravestone is on the right as you enter the village cemetery, set slightly apart from the headstones of seven RAF Volunteer Reserve personnel from 10 Squadron who died when their Halifax bomber came down on the night of 16 July 1943. It is possible to visit the crash site, where a small memorial has been erected, although it is off the beaten track. Follow the sign *'Stele des Anglais'* that leads north from the cemetery into some woods. The road becomes a track. Turn left at **GPS 47.799955, 4.860822** and continue for another half a mile towards the farm called Mont de Lucey. If you are travelling in a vehicle, continue on foot along a path that descends to the right towards some woods. The memorial is on the edge of these woods (**GPS 47.795334, 4.848170**).

Lieutenant Mike Pinci

On 23/24 August Lieutenant Mike Pinci and his section parachuted into the area just south of the village of Les Goulles (**GPS 47.866119, 4.900247**), approximately 10 miles north of Recey-sur-Ource on the D102C. He was killed, however, just east of the village, strafed by an American P-47 on the afternoon of 11 September. Head east on the D928 towards Colmier-le-Haut. After approximately 2 miles you will see a turning to the left signposted Gurgy-le-Chateau (**GPS 47.790286, 4.888955**). Close by was where Pinci was killed.

A large memorial on which Pinci's name is engraved can be found just to the east of Auberive on the RN428, also known as the Route de Langres (**GPS 47.785072, 5.068357**). The memorial ostensibly commemorates members of the local Maquis who were killed fighting to liberate their country, but Pinci and another officer, an Anglo-Swiss man called Jocelyn Radice, are listed under 'Captaines Anglais' (although the latter's Christian name has been misspelt as 'Jocelin'). Captain Radice was a member of the Jedburgh 'Bunny' Team, along with Sergeant Jim Chambers and Lieutenant Maurice Géminel. On 20 August the trio encountered a German convoy as they passed through the town of Plesnoy. In the ensuing shootout, Radice, a member of Blackheath rugby club and a veteran of the North African campaign, was shot in the left knee. He was brought back to the farm where his Jedburgh team was based, but the limited medical supplies were inadequate to treat his serious wound. It

The memorial to the Maquis on which are the names of Mike Pinci and Jocelyn Radice, the latter's Christian name misspelt.

became gangrenous and Radice was taken to Langres hospital, where he died despite the best efforts of the Maquis surgeon to save his life.

Radice and Pinci were initially interred at Auberive village cemetery, but their bodies were exhumed after the war and their final resting place is the Clichy Northern Cemetery in Paris (**GPS 48.907480, 2.315205**).

Giey-sur-Aujon Churchyard
From the site of Pinci's death, continue east on the D928 (which becomes the D428) as far as Colmier-le-Haut, and then take the D102K north to Giey-sur-Aujon. This village is where, on 23 August, an SAS patrol ran into a detachment of White Russians in Nazi uniform. The churchyard (**GPS 47.905643, 5.068121**) is where Lieutenant Dayrell Morris first spotted the Russians among the gravestones. A grenade followed and the fleeing Russians were then cut down by a burst of fire from the SAS jeep.

Villaines-les-Prévôtes
On the same day that the men of Operation Hardy were battling Russians in Giey-sur-Aujon, 57 miles to the south-west the rest of C Squadron were approaching the village of Villaines-les-Prévôtes. Captain Ramon Lee was in

the vanguard, followed by the jeep of Lieutenant Lord John Manners, with Roy Farran's column nearly an hour behind.

Lee approached the village from the south-west, along the present-day D103M, and the initial contact with the Germans occurred at the t-junction of the Rue Aveu and the Place de la Fontaine (**GPS 47.554230, 4.30519**). The two jeeps turned sharp left, up Place de la Fontaine, which is a cul-du-sac. If in a car, alight here, and walk up the cul-du-sac and imagine that dramatic evening of 23 August as Len Rudd braked hard, realising he was in a dead end. Rudd met his end on the steps to the right, probably as he sought shelter in the house. The village mayor, Monsieur Vailliard, did not specify in his statement that Rudd was shot, only that he was 'killed in falling', but presumably he was. Valliard also stated that the Germans 'despoiled' his body. This probably entailed searching the dead soldier for any papers or clues to his unit's identity, and doubtless removing any cigarettes. The Germans in Villaines-les-Prévôtes belonged to the Afrika Korps, and it is unlikely they would have desecrated Rudd's body in the way the SS violated Thomas Bintley's (see Chapter 1). There was a strong mutual respect between the SAS and the Afrika Korps, and when in April 1945 several 1SAS soldiers were captured by the Afrika Korps in Germany, they were well treated and the veterans among them reminisced about the war in North Africa.

Rudd's comrades, including Captain Lee and Lieutenant Manners, escaped into the field at the end of the Place de la Fontaine, where today stands a large iron gate.

This is the cul-de-sac into which the SAS drove in Villaines. Rudd died on the steps to the right, and his comrades escaped into the field at the back.

Rudd along with the other fatality of the fight at Villaines-les-Prévôtes, Ron McEachan, were buried in the churchyard after a service conducted by the village priest. 'The whole population attended the funeral and covered the coffin [the pair were buried in a single coffin],' remarked the mayor. 'We propose to make an enclosure round their tomb. 'They may have done so but after the war McEachan and Rudd subsequently received official CWGC headstones. They are unmissable as you enter the pretty churchyard of Villaines-les-Prévôtes (**GPS 47.555320, 4.305918**), their upkeep the proud responsibility of *La Confédération Nationale des Combattants volontaires de la Résistance.*

In 2004 Rudd's nephew visited his uncle's grave for the first time, and he met some of the villagers. One, a young woman visiting her family from her university in Paris, explained that 'the 23rd August 1944 was their war. Villaines-les-Prévôtes was so out of the way that from 1939 until their liberation in September 1944 they had rarely seen a German . . . it was not until that day in August 1944 when the Afrika Korps and the SAS had come to town that the war touched them.'

Standing in the lane that leads to the churchyard from the village, one can look west across the field and get an idea of the SAS escape route as they fled from the Place de la Fontaine. Two soldiers who didn't get away were Lieutenant Ralph Dodds and Lance Corporal Stan Walsh. Neither reported

The graves of Rudd and McEachan, still lovingly tended by the villagers. Interestingly, McEachan's grave does not mention the SAS.

mistreatment from the Afrika Korps and, given the fate meted out to dozens of captured SAS soldiers in 1944, the pair were fortunate that they fell into the hands of honourable soldiers.

The Afrika Korps withdrew that evening, taking their prisoners with them, as they made for Dijon. Dodds and Walsh were handed over in the city and, along with scores of other Allied prisoners, herded into a train bound for Germany. The train departed on 2 September but only a few miles east of Dijon it was attacked by American fighter aircraft. Several prisoners and guards were killed but those POWs who survived were able to escape into the countryside. Dodds and Walsh had been separated on the train because of their rank and the latter was unable to find his officer. 'As he was almost unable to walk, owing to an injury to his ankle, I do not believe that he got away from the train,' wrote Walsh in a statement shortly after he was repatriated to England in October 1944. For many months the fate of Ralph Dodds remained a source of alarm for 2SAS but in fact he had continued his journey to Germany, where he spent the rest of the war in Oflag 79. He remained in the army post-war, retiring with the rank of lieutenant colonel in the Intelligence Corps in 1969.

Not long after Dodds and Walsh had been captured, Farran's patrol approached Villaines-les-Prévôtes. According to the mayor, when the SAS were 100 metres from the village 'the Germans signalled their approach and fired a cannon at the first vehicle, which collapsed in the ditch and the

Looking towards the entry to Villaines, this is the bank on which Clarke and Carpendale sited their Bren.

occupants fled'. This was Farran's jeep and the ditch it drove into is the one opposite the bank on the left of the road (**GPS 47.551417, 4.301541**). Up this bank scrambled Corporal Clarke and Lieutenant Brian 'Chips' Carpendale with a Bren gun. Further down the road were the jeeps of Lieutenant Jim Mackie and Harry Vickers. They pulled off right into the track that runs at right angles to the D103M road into Villaines-les-Prévôtes (**GPS 47.549971, 4.302105**).

Vickers' section took up position on the right of the road (D103M), concealed behind the hedgerow, and from here they were able to inflict heavy casualties on the Afrika Korps as they advanced south across the field. A short while later the SAS came under mortar and machine-gun fire from Germans who had worked their way behind them to a point approximately at **GPS 47.552282, 4.308007** on the Rue du Patis.

Farran ordered their withdrawal and they headed south-west on the D103M, traversing what today is the D1 until they reached the mill (**GPS 47.543540, 4.284117**), which today is the Poney Club du Moulin. Now, as in August 1944, the road is a dead-end so Farran and his men went cross-country, bouncing in their jeeps south-west across fields for a mile and a half until they reached the village of Jeux-lès-Bard. From here they continued towards Operation Hardy's base in the forest of Châtillon.

An hour or so later Lieutenant Gurney led his section down the same road to the mill, carrying with them the mortally wounded David Leigh and the

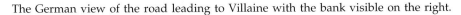

The German view of the road leading to Villaine with the bank visible on the right.

body of Ron McEachan. They left the body of McEachan on the track 200 metres from the mill, where he was found by the French. 'There were no identification materials on him but certain papers made it appear that was he was a radio-telegraphist,' reported the mayor. 'The papers of the soldier were probably taken by his comrades who should have given news of the matter.'

Époisses

David Leigh died shortly after he was brought inside a house in Époisses, and he was buried in the village cemetery (**GPS 47.509204, 4.176393**). There is parking at the front of the cemetery, although when I visited, the front gate to the cemetery was locked. There is a side entrance and close by on the wall is a map showing the location of Leigh's gravestone. David and his younger brother Tom had been orphaned in their adolescence. Tom, a pilot officer in the RAF, had been shot down in 1941 and was for nearly three years a POW until, on the night of 24/25 March 1944, he escaped from Stalag Luft III along with seventy-five other men. For several days he fled on foot through the Lower Silesia countryside before being recaptured. On 31 March Tom and

David and Ethel at their wedding. Three months later he was dead. Ethel died in 2010 and her ashes were interred with her husband's body.

five other failed escapees were marched into woods near Görlitz and shot, six of the fifty victims of the 'Great Escape' immortalised in the Hollywood film of 1963.

David's wife of twelve weeks, Ethel, never remarried. She died in February 2010 and at her request her ashes were interred with her husband's body in a service attended by scores of villagers.

Bierry-les-Belles-Fontaines

Having left David Leigh at Époisses, the SAS contingent, under the command of Ramon Lee, drove north and approached the village of Bierry-les-Belles-Fontaines at about midnight. They entered from the south (**GPS 47.594978, 4.178897**), driving down the rue de Vassey, before turning left onto the Rue des Chaudronniers. After 100 metres this road bears right and it was at the farm of Monsieur Cadoux (**GPS 47.598433, 4.182775**) that the SAS were fired on by a German sentry, the bullet grazing the head of Lieutenant Edmund Birtwistle in the lead jeep. Lee ordered his men to dismount from their four vehicles but Sergeant Pete Tomasso, who was behind the wheel in the last in the column, reversed back up the rue de Vassey.

When I visited Bierry-les-Belles-Fontaines in September 2020 I met Maurice Rousselet, a local historian, who still recalled vividly the June day in 1940

The rue de Vassey in Bierry-les-Belles-Fontaines, up which the SAS reversed to escape the German fire.

Maurice Rousselet at his home in Bierry-les-Belles-Fontaines in 2020 with a replica SAS jeep, similar to the ones which entered his village on the evening of 23 August.

2SAS reunion, circa 1960s: (*left to right*) Bob Young, Horace Stokes, George Daniels, Jack Rooks, Tim Robinson, Larry Browneless and Harry Vickers.

when the Germans entered his village and installed themselves in the Château d'Anstrude (**GPS 47.595655, 4.183585**). In 1944 he was a farmhand, and he recalled finishing a long day in the fields on 23 August to learn from an excited villager that the English 'in funny little vehicles' were fighting the Germans in Villaines-les-Prévôtes.

Châtillon-sur-Seine

The Battle of Châtillon-sur-Seine is remembered annually in the town and for many years the ceremony was attended by 2SAS veterans who had beaten back the Nazis on 30 August 1944. The pilgrimage across the Channel began in earnest in 1980, coinciding – as with other SAS trips to France – with the veterans reaching retirement age. With more time on their hands, they began to reflect on the heroic exploits of their salad days. Ten veterans visited Châtillon-sur-Seine in 1980, part of a trip that included a reception at the Château d'Anstrude in Bierry-les-Belles-Fontaines and services at the gravesides of those of their comrades who had been killed on Hardy/Wallace.

Two years later, on 20 June 1982, the SAS veterans were back in force to witness the inauguration of a memorial to Bill Holland, who was killed on the Pont du Seine on 30 August 1944. Among the pilgrims were Roy Farran, Harry Vickers, Charlie Hackney and Tanky Challenor. The memorial (**GPS 47.856060, 4.568451**) is a few yards from the spot where Holland was mortally

The memorial to Bill Holland on the south side of the bridge, inaugurated in 1982, doesn't stand on the site where he fell.

CHATILLON-sur-SEINE (Côte-d'Or)
Parc et Château Marmont où résida le Généralissime Joffre
en Septembre 1914, pendant la glorieuse bataille de la Marne

Château Marmont and its impressive gates through which the Germans poured as the SAS attack began.

wounded. He then staggered back up the Avenue Maréchal Joffre towards the roundabout but collapsed outside No. 4 (**GPS 47.856806, 4.570976**). Carried inside by Monsieur and Madame Bienaime, Holland died on the floor of their house.

The bridge on which Harry Vickers positioned his section – the Pont du Seine – has been rebuilt post-war, and the rue du Montbard has been widened and modernised. Nonetheless, standing on the bridge one can easily get a sense of the tension the SAS must have felt as they gazed south at the approaching German column.

Lieutenant Jim Mackie was situated on what today is the Place Joffre roundabout (**GPS 47.856940, 4.571590**), the ideal position to direct the firefight on the bridge. The Germans never made any progress along the rue de Montbard, and the fiercest exchanges were to the north at the Place Marmont (**GPS 47.861393, 4.574691**) as the Germans attacked along the Rue Marmont from their HQ at the château of the same name (**GPS 47.864353, 4.567499**).

The château is not open to the public and it is not possible to go any further from the gates on Rue de l'Abbaye (**GPS 47.862898, 4.571138**), but it was from here that the Nazis advanced towards the SAS on the Place Marmont.

Farran in his report was critical of the fact that the Maquis did not show at the agreed time on 30 August, and certainly the mutual respect that existed, for example, between 1SAS in the Morvan and their local Maquis did not exist on Operation Hardy/Wallace. Nonetheless, it should be borne in mind that two months before 2SAS arrived the poorly equipped Maquis had suffered heavy losses when they were attacked by an estimated 2,000 Germans.

In the days after the invasion, hundreds of eager young men had flocked to the forest of Châtillon, where for many months a Maquis force of approximately 150 had been based, swelling the numbers to around 500. Needless to say, the Germans swiftly learned of their presence and launched an attack on 10 June supported by White Russians. Thirty-seven Maquisards were killed, several after undergoing brutal torture, and the capture of what arms and equipment they possessed was a severe blow to the already under-manned Maquis. There is an imposing memorial to the dead men, deep in the forest of Châtillon, close to the scene of the heaviest fighting. In addition to the monument there is a large information map which, although in French, loses little in translation as it pinpoints sites of interest in the surrounding area that make up the 'The Remembrance Trail'. This includes a few of the SAS memorials. To reach the Resistance monument, take the D16 south-west from Châtillon-sur-Seine for 8 miles into the heart of the forest. The memorial, which is well signposted, is at **GPS 47.791789, 4.681263**.

Hennezel
Outside the boundary of 'The Remembrance Trail' is the DZ where, on 6/7 September, Roy Farran's troop was attacked by 600 SS troops shortly after

Lieutenant Hugh Gurney, Lance Corporal Tanky Challenor and Private Bob Fyfe had arrived by parachute.

In his report on the attack, which included four armoured cars, six troop carriers and twenty staff cars, Farran omitted a map reference for the DZ, so therefore it is impossible to pinpoint its exact location. He did, however, mention a deep stream that flowed across the field and blocked their escape route north and west. This might be the Ruisseau de Thiétry – a 'ruisseau' being a stream – which flows north-west before curving south-west, and so **GPS 48.049797, 6.095709** could be a rough approximation of the location of the DZ. Furthermore, south-west of this spot is a track, like the one mentioned by Farran, along which they drove until they reached the main road (**GPS 48.051059, 6.112489**), which today is the D5D.

What is certain is that, having escaped the Nazi ambush, the SAS then carried out one of their own at Hennezel (**GPS 48.053321, 6.116399**), led by the redoubtable Sergeant Vickers, which killed two high-ranking SS officers. Vickers returned to Hennezel in 1994 for a 50th anniversary commemoration. 'An old man came up to me and said that on the morning of the shooting three young soldiers had stopped at his house,' recalled Vickers. 'I said that I was one of them. He looked a bit doubtful, so I said that we had parked the jeep outside his house and when we came back the villagers had hung wreaths of dahlias around our guns. The French civilians were a bit too exuberant really, but it was quite understandable.'

Velorcey

A few days after the Hennezel incident, on 11 September the SAS attempted another ambush against the Nazis but this attack went tragically awry. Lieutenant Hugh Gurney's two jeeps arrived at the village of Velorcey from the north, along the track known today as the En Bobenoz (**GPS 47.780920, 6.250959**). They continued south through the village on the Grande Rue until they reached the t-junction at the Route de Luxeuil (**GPS 47.777887, 6.251048**). Gurney positioned his jeeps on either side of the junction, with his own vehicle on the eastern side, looking down the Route de Luxeuil in the direction of Abelcourt. It was from this direction that the German column arrived and Gurney and his men opened fire when the lead vehicle, an ammunition truck, was 10 yards away. When the truck exploded, Gurney and Tanky Challenor were rendered insensible by the force of the blast. Gurney was shot dead as he and Challenor staggered across the t-junction towards the second jeep. Evidence of the explosion can still be seen in the pockmarked walls of some of the buildings on the Route de Luxeuil.

The Germans initially refused to let Gurney be laid to rest because they considered him a 'terrorist', so his body was left on the side of the road for two days. On 13 September the villagers of Velorcey buried him in their churchyard, and here he lies still, the only war grave in the small churchyard

(**GPS 47.780129, 6.250846**). In the summer of 1962 Tanky Challenor drove down through France to pay his respects to his former officer. 'I was made welcome by the people of the village and I was happy to see Mr Gurney's grave was freshly adorned with flowers,' he wrote in an article for the SAS journal, *Mars and Minerva*. 'I sat in the village schoolroom and I thought "He stood for everything that was fine and decent" … I was very proud of him.'

There is also inside the church of Velorcey a memorial plaque in honour of the 'Englishman' Gurney, 'who died for France'.

James Downey's grave

Private James Downey's is the only war grave in the cemetery at Terre-Natale Communal Cemetery on the northern side of the village of Varennes-sur-Amance (**GPS 47.898955, 5.627568**).

Ambush site

Operation Wallace wound down a few days after the deaths of Mike Pinci, Hugh Gurney and James Downey, but not before Captain Bob Walker-Brown had carried out an effective ambush on a German convoy of petrol bowsers. Siting the ambush on the advice of the Maquis 'at a point where the country road crossed the main road', the SAS allowed the escort vehicles to pass un-molested before opening up on the bowsers. The SAS men were positioned on a small bank alongside what today is the D3 (**GPS 47.980966, 4.894785**) and the bowsers were destroyed as they drove south towards Châtillon-sur-Seine on the D65. Walker-Brown recalled that they were attacked in the rear by the escort vehicles, which had presumably turned left along the track that turns off the D65 (**GPS 47.976405, 4.891395**) and came round behind the SAS.

Choloy War Cemetery

Bill Holland was buried far from where he fell, in the British war cemetery at Choloy, 100 miles north-east of Châtillon-sur-Seine and 15 miles east of the city of Nancy (**GPS 48.666553, 5.850548**). The cemetery, which contains nearly 500 burials from the 1939–1945 war, is next to a large French one from the First World War. As usual, the register will guide you to the gravestone of Bill Holland. There are two other SAS men in this cemetery, Edward Drew of 2SAS, who was killed in an accident during Operation Wallace/Hardy, and Keith Robertson of 1SAS, who was a member of Operation Kipling, and who lost his life in a road traffic accident. Interestingly Robertson's grave has no cross, which is unusual.

The grave of Bill Holland, one of three SAS men in Choloy war cemetery.

Chapter Four

Operation Loyton

Six days before Roy Farran and his men embarked on Operation Wallace, another 2SAS operation was launched. Codenamed Loyton, it was centred on the Vosges, approximately 100 miles north-east of the Plateau de Langres. Originally, as Loyton's operational report admitted, 'it had been hoped to mount this operation shortly before or immediately after D-day, at a time when the area was relatively lightly held by enemy forces and while there were in France many other areas of partisan activity which would distract enemy attention from the presence of S.A.S. troops in so sensitive a position astride their main communications with the Reich.'

But there was a problem to that plan, namely that 38 Group RAF was 'unable to despatch men or supplies to this area until the beginning of the longer hours of darkness in August'. So Loyton was suspended and then resurrected in August, but with a new mission, one which would exploit the success achieved by the swift American Third Army advance across France after the breakout from Normandy. The SAS were to operate against the main railway lines running westwards from Strasbourg (including Metz and Nancy), and additionally attack soft transport on the road network. 'The recce party will be followed by reinforcements,' ran the operational instruction. 'If this party were successful and targets were available and aircraft supply problems proved easy, permission to increase the party up to one squadron would almost certainly be given.' The confident tone of the instruction belied the hazardous area into which the men of A Squadron, 2SAS, were to be inserted. Only 100 miles separated Loyton from Wallace, but they could have been in different countries.

First there was the terrain. The Vosges are a range of hills running north to south on the French side of the river Rhine. There is a Brothers Grimm feel to the forests that carpet the hills, thick, dark and mysterious, harbouring who knows what inside. Narrow roads wind around the hills and valleys, cutting through villages and alongside rivers and gorges. It is ideal country for guerrilla warfare.

Secondly, unlike the Plateau de Langres or the Massif du Morvan, however, the latter the rich hunting ground for 1SAS in Operation Houndsworth, the Vosges were inhabited by people whose loyalty to the Allies was dubious. 'The population of Alsace had closer racial ties with the Germans, while most of the purely French inhabitants of Lorraine had been deported to southern France or the Reich itself,' ran a report by the SAS Brigade. 'Moreover German control over administration was tighter and more direct in preparation for the eventual incorporation of the provinces into the Grosse-Deutschland.' Nonetheless, those villagers whose allegiance was to France – more often than not those on the western side of the Vosges – were fiercely proud of their country and hated the Nazi Occupiers with an intensity surpassing that of their compatriots in other regions in France who hadn't been embittered by the experience of German intrusion.

Thirdly, the German troops in the Vosges were not as demoralised and disorganised as those further west, from where they were withdrawing. In the Vosges the Nazis were well equipped and well fed and determined to defend what they considered their homeland.

There was also a strong Gestapo presence in the form of the BDS (Befehlshaber der Sicherheitpolizei), which had its own force in Alsace separate from the BDS France. In charge of the BDS Alsace was Standartenführer Dr Erich Isselhorst, who had arrived in Strasbourg in January 1944. A lawyer who had joined the Gestapo in 1935, Isselhorst had risen up the ranks after his success in dealing with Russian partisans. He was described subsequently by the 2SAS Intelligence officer Eric Barkworth as 'intelligent but gives the impression of weak character and inefficiency'. His deputy commander was Wilhelm Schneider, a bald man with a white goatee beard and a thin, craggy face. Formerly a merchant seaman, he found a new vocation in the Nazi Party. 'Pompous, ineffective and fond of drink', Schneider found an outlet for his latent brutality in the Gestapo.

BDS France was based in Nancy, Lorraine, 80 miles west of Strasbourg, although its units only arrived in the city from Paris on approximately 15 August. They brought with them 'a secret order … to the effect that all parachutists captured behind the lines were to be shot within 48 hours'.

Loyton was planned to be 'operationally complementary to the Maquis activity' although the SAS were to maintain their separate organisation throughout the operation. The man selected to lead the SAS advance party was Captain Henry Druce, although it was a last-minute appointment after the officer initially chosen lost his nerve on the eve of departure. In desperation, Brian Franks turned to Druce, who had only recently joined the regiment after some outstanding service with MI6 earlier in the war. He had much to recommend him: fluent in French, Flemish and Dutch, Druce was bold, ruthless and unflappable. 'With the men standing by the aircraft I was telephoned in Scotland and told to rush down to Fairford,' remembered Druce. He brought with him his sergeant, Ralph 'Jock' Hay, whose qualities mirrored those of his officer.

Druce arrived at Fairford on 12 August and was briefed on the operation and introduced to the three-man Jedburgh team, whose codename was Jacob.

In the front row of this photo taken in Italy in December 1943 are Ralph Hay (*left*) and Lieutenant Jimmy Hughes. They joined 2SAS together from the Royal Artillery.

A word about the 'Jeds', who were attached to SAS operations in France in 1944 and who, in the main, were a valuable asset. They were in effect the middlemen between the Maquis and SHAEF (Supreme Headquarters Allied Expeditionary Force), working alongside the SAS in coordinating guerrilla actions against the Nazis. The Jedburgh Directive of 20 December 1943 stated that they should 'provide a strategic reserve for creating and controlling offensive action behind enemy lines on and after D-Day where existing communications, leadership, organisation, or supplies are inadequate, and for carrying out specific tasks demanded by the military situation'.

Composed of approximately 300 volunteers, their name derived from the Scottish market town in the rolling Border countryside where the Jedburghs did much of their training. Prior to their physical and technical training each man underwent a thorough assessment by an army psychiatrist. The Jedburgh HQ was situated at the Special Forces Headquarters (SFHQ) in Baker Street, London. Each team comprised three members, usually (but not always) a British member of SOE, an American from the Office of Strategic Services (OSS) and a Frenchman from the Central Bureau of Intelligence and Action (BCRA). Of these three one was a radio operator.

That role in Team Jacob – the 26th 'Jed' team to be inserted into France – was performed by Sergeant Ken Seymour (see Chapter 5). Its leader was Captain Victor Gough and its deputy Lieutenant Guy Baraud, whose real name was Maurice Boissarie. Gough and Boissarie were friends as well as comrades; the Frenchman, born in Bordeaux in 1914, was four years Gough's senior, and before the war had been an insurance inspector. Gough was from the west of England, a mechanical engineer with a flair for illustrations. He enlisted in the Somerset Light Infantry and volunteered for SOE in 1943, where he was deployed initially as a training officer before becoming operational shortly before D-Day. Gough had won a competition to design the wings that each Jedburgh man wore.

The advance party commanded by Druce left RAF Fairford in Gloucestershire in two aircraft on the evening of 12/13 August. There were fifteen men in total, along with numerous containers packed with equipment, rations and over 200 weapons with which to arm the local Maquis.

'I had passed through the Vosges before the war so I had a general idea of what the place looked like,' recalled Druce. 'I thought what we were being asked to do was possible; but it was made clear to me in the briefing that I wasn't to go around blowing things up. My job as the advance party was to reconnoitre the area and establish a good DZ for the main party, to select suitable targets [for later action] and to contact the Maquis.'

Among the 2SAS personnel was Ronald Crossfield, better known as 'Dusty', an 'old sweat' who had joined the army in 1934 and whose seven brothers were all in uniform. 'All lights were doused as we approached the coast and I remember that as we flew over my home town, Brighton, [I was] thinking about my wife and three-year-old son down there and wondering whether this was going to be a one way trip,' he reflected. 'A tot of rum each warmed us up just before we got the order to "Hook up".'

Crossfield shuffled into line behind Captain John Hislop, leader of a three-man Phantom signalling patrol. The 33-year-old Hislop had an unusual background. A noted jockey before the war, he was a veteran of Dunkirk and

Philippe and Maurice Boissarie. Maurice jumped into the Vosges as part of Jedburgh's Team Jacob and was killed a few weeks later.

joined Phantom to escape what he regarded as the cliques of a traditional regiment. He subsequently volunteered for 2SAS because he was on good terms with Bill Stirling, an aficionado of horse racing.

'Phantom' teams were responsible for radio communications support on SAS missions (whereas Jedburgh teams liaised with the Maquis and SOE agents). More formally known as F Squadron, GHQ Liaison Regiment, Phantom's commander was Major the Honourable Jakie Astor. One of the early members was Sergeant Arthur Wood, who recalled that the squadron was looking for a purpose in late 1943 when a call came for volunteers to undergo a parachute course. 'Having no idea what our ultimate role would be, all 80 of us stepped forward, and so still as "F" we found ourselves back in Scotland, this time at Auchinleck in Ayrshire. Here a PE instructor had to toughen us up before we began our parachute training ... back in Auchinleck we were put into patrols of five – an officer, an NCO and three wireless operators – and sent to various squadrons of the SAS. "F" Squadron became SAS Phantom, and our role was to provide signals for this very special service.'

Each Phantom patrol had a regular listening period throughout the day in Occupied France when they would tune in for the SABU broadcasts, SABU being the codename for the SAS broadcasts that were emitted to all squadrons operating in Occupied France. Each SABU had a number that corresponded to the Phantom Patrols so they would know when the message was for them. Each broadcast from England commenced with the tune 'Sur le pont d'Avignon', a popular French song. Phantom operators required not only a high degree of skill but also diligence and self-discipline to ensure they never missed a broadcast despite the often exacting circumstances in which they were operating deep inside enemy territory.

Probably the most vital facet of the Phantom patrol's work was liaising with HQ about resupply. 'It worked that in the morning I would receive a message such as 'One plane, ten containers to blue DZ, estimated time of arrival 0100 hours, running in from north to south, recognition letter P. Acknowledge,' explained Wood, who was attached to 1SAS. 'About half an hour before time of arrival I would take another operator up to the DZ with my "Eureka", which worked to the "Rebecca" in the plane. If a plane flew over and I didn't get a high-pitched noise through my headphones I would let it go. When I did get the high-pitch I would light up a small flare path with sand soaked in petrol and the supplies would be dropped by parachute.'

Captain Druce and the advance party jumped at 0200 hours on 13 August. 'Not the best landing for me as I could see that I was drifting towards the trees and pulling hard on my rigging lines didn't help,' said Crossfield. 'Both helmet and kitbag were wrenched off as I crashed through the branches and came to rest swinging gently with no idea of the distance between me and the ground. I punched my quick release and dropped heavily to the deck – it must have been about 15 feet. Someone was running towards me and I reckon I had my [colt] 45 out faster than John Wayne, but the cry of "Tres Bien, Angleterre" saved the lad from being shot. I fared better than some: Captain Druce had concussion and Ginger [Wally Hall] had damaged his knee so it was a slow march to cover the 9 miles to the first camp.'

Also injured was the Jedburgh wireless operator, Sergeant Ken Seymour, who 'seriously damaged the big toe of my left foot which necessitated my moving about without a shoe'. Seymour was helped off the DZ by 20-year-old Henri Poirson, a local lorry driver for a company providing 'essential'

Henry Druce, seen here shortly after the war, joined Loyton at the last minute but proved himself a shrewd and audacious officer.

services to the population. Organised by the mayor of the village of Moussey, Jules Py, the company was also a means of employing young men, thereby making them ineligible for STO (*Service du travail obligatoire*). This was a forced labour scheme introduced in France by the Nazis in 1942 that resulted in the deportation of hundreds of thousands of French workers to Germany to work for their war effort.

For many months Poirson had moonlighted for the Maquis, using his lorry to transport shot-down Allied airmen and other personnel crucial to the war effort to safe houses on an escape line that ultimately would lead to Britain.

The containers were harvested by the Maquis, whose chief was Colonel 'Maximum', and later on 13 August he hosted a conference for his visitors. Druce discovered that the French had appropriated the arms as 'more or less the price arranged for the use of their field', but since this had been the plan he wasn't too perturbed, particularly as the Maquis were happy to feed and shelter them for the time being.

Their camp, codenamed A, was deep in the forest 5 miles north of Moussey, on the Col des Marcassins. 'It consisted of wooden huts made from cut-down trees on top of the hill in a good defensive position,' wrote Druce. 'The camp seemed well organised and well run, and the Maquis in this camp consisted of about eighty men who previously had about ten to fifteen assorted old and rusty rifles.'

On 15 August the SAS learned that a large force of Germans, possibly as many as 5,000, had moved into a neighbouring valley. This was more troubling news for Druce, who was already finding the Maquis leadership somewhat erratic. His pressing task was to source a suitable DZ for the main party but he was no closer to achieving this aim 48 hours after arriving.

It was decided to move to a new base, codenamed B, situated in the forest at a place known locally as Jardin David, approximately 1½ miles to the south-east. Druce divided his party in two and set off on 17 August. With him – as well as a number of Maquis – went the Phantom signallers and the Jedburgh team, while a French captain called Goodfellow was given command of four SAS men comprising Crossfield, Hay, Wally 'Ginger' Hall and 36-year-old Robert Lodge. Their orders were to depart the camp on 18 August. Hall was a former Grenadier Guardsman, as his father had been, and was popular among his peers for his friendly and cheerful disposition. Nonetheless, recalled Hislop, he possessed 'an innate sense of military duty'. Lodge was actually Rudolf Friedlaender, a German Jew who with his family had fled his country in the 1930s and settled in Twickenham. Despite being significantly

Wally Hall (*second right*), known as 'Ginger', was a Guardsman who took well to irregular warfare.

older than the average SAS trooper – and requiring glasses for his short-sightedness – Lodge was described by Hislop as 'a first-class soldier'.

In addition, Lew Fiddick, a shot-down Canadian airman, a bomb aimer on a Lancaster, who had been brought to Druce by the Maquis on 15 August, was attached to the second party. Fiddick's aircraft had been shot down in the early hours of 29 July after being attacked by a Messerschmitt 110 en route to a raid on Stuttgart. Three of the crew were killed by the Nazi fighter's cannon fire but Fiddick and three others baled out. One, the British flight engineer George Wishart, was badly injured on landing and required hospital treatment. That saved his life. The other two, Canadians and buddies of Fiddick's, pilot Al Peabody and navigator Harry Doe, parachuted safely to earth but were captured a few hours later and subsequently murdered by the Nazis. Their bodies have never been found.

Lodge was leading the patrol through the forest when he froze and signalled for the men following to do likewise. 'Suddenly all hell broke loose and everyone dived flat,' remembered Crossfield. 'Schmeissers, Lugers and rifles were all firing at us. We retaliated with our Brens and carbines. I know I used up three magazines very quickly. The Germans, firing through thick scrub, were not more than 30 yards away. They could not see us but we heard a scream or two.'

While Lodge kept the Germans at bay with shorts bursts from the Bren gun, Goodfellow, who was in reality a Frenchman called Robert de Lesseps, a grandson of the man who constructed the Suez Canal, ordered the men to withdraw. Crossfield began to crawl back through the trees and saw Ginger Hall lying wounded. 'I went to drag him away but he moaned "Leave me, I've had it. Get away." He had been hit twice in the chest and we had no choice but to leave him.' As Crossfield and the rest of the patrol withdrew safely through the trees, they could hear the chatter of Lodge's Bren, growing ever fainter the further they moved away. Eventually the forest fell quiet.

Druce, meanwhile, had also encountered some trouble. 'It was when we were on the move to this second camp that we saw the German patrol coming,' he remembered. 'We got off the pathway, below it, instead of being brighter and going above it so we'd have a superior situation.' As they moved off the path into the woods a shot rang out. 'That started the silly situation,' said Druce. 'We were strung out over perhaps 200 yards with all these unarmed Frenchmen with Germans sitting above you, shooting down at you. Didn't have a chance.'

Druce had furnished his men with a map reference rendezvous and instructed them to make their way there. Two never showed at the rendezvous: Sergeant Seymour of the Jedburgh team and Sergeant Gerald Davis of the Phantom Patrol.

There were repercussions for the 1,200 inhabitants of Moussey after the skirmish in the woods. On 18 August fifty-four men, including the gendarmes and the forest wardens, were arrested. They were taken first to the BDS HQ at the Belval château, built at the turn of the century in a neo-renaissance style. During the First World War it had been occupied by the Germans and a quarter of a century later it was once more in their hands. The day before the attack on the SAS, a new unit had arrived at the Belval château, the Kommando Schöner, composed of thirty men under the command of Erwin Schöner, who answered directly to Wilhelm Schneider. To augment the Kommando Schöner, a Wehrmacht unit was attached to them, commanded by Major Reisser. Of the fifty-four men arrested at Moussey on 18 August forty-four were deported and only eight returned at the end of the war.

Druce and Goodfellow were reunited on 23 August and three days later they were scheduled to welcome a ten-strong reinforcement party under Major Peter Power but a breakdown in communication resulted in the new group landing 25 miles west of the DZ. 'We were feeling very depressed and helpless,' remarked Druce in his operational report. 'And with a strong temptation of going off and shooting up what we could find.'

Power was the commanding officer of A Squadron, and his second-in-command was Lieutenant Alastair McGregor, a superb guerrilla soldier, who had established this reputation during operations in Italy the previous winter. Together, the stick began the trek eastwards towards the original DZ but in early September they split up when Power received a message from Brigade HQ instructing them to blow up a stretch of railway line. McGregor and four men attempted to carry out their orders to the best of their ability but, low on

Moussey, seen here between the wars, paid a heavy price for its fidelity to the SAS and the Maquis.

169 — MOUSSEY
Vallée du Harcholet

explosives and rations, they accomplished little before eventually reaching American lines on 8 October. Power and his men finally arrived at the main Loyton base on 17 September.

On the night of 30/31 August Lieutenant Colonel Brian Franks and twenty-three men parachuted onto a hastily arranged DZ. Druce was in a heightened state of alert, aware of rumours of many Germans in the vicinity. Not that this seemed to worry the Maquis unduly. 'I was met on the DZ by Capt. Druce and also by a large number of Frenchmen making an almost un-believable noise,' wrote Franks in his report. 'Capt. Druce, however, appeared to have the situation under control and the removal of containers etc. from the D.Z. was, to start with, well organised. However, after we had been there about an hour and a half there was considerable shouting and shooting and I was told that the Germans had attacked, which news did not surprise me in view of the noise made by the French.'

Druce described the scene as 'pandemonium'. In fact what had happened was a Maquis prisoner had tried to escape as his guards helped themselves to the contents of the containers. One of the guards was a Russian deserter from the German army and he shouted 'Achtung'. On hearing the word, the rest of the Maquis thought they were under attack and opened fire. Order was eventually restored and the prisoner recaptured. Anxious to avoid a

Brian Franks (*left*) assumed command of 2SAS from Bill Stirling and proved an astute and brave CO.

repetition, Druce had him shot. He wasn't the only fatality on this chaotic evening; another Russian, excitedly opening a container, found a slab of plastic explosive and stuffed it into his mouth in the belief it was actually food. As a result of the arsenic in the explosive he died what Druce recalled was 'a most uncomfortable death'.

Along with Franks had parachuted Captains Anthony Whatley-Smith and Christopher Sykes. The latter was 2SAS's intelligence officer and also a good friend of Evelyn Waugh, the novelist. A Francophile, Sykes was more sympathetic towards the Maquis than most of his peers. Describing those on the DZ as 'untrained, unarmed, expectant and physically exhausted young men, whose only idea of military formation was to assemble in large masses', he nonetheless recognised their innate courage and their determination to rid their land of the Nazis.

Franks arrived in the Vosges at the moment the Allied advance lost momentum. So rapid had their drive east been that the Americans overstretched their supply chain and the battlefield became temporarily static. The Germans were in dire need of a respite and they used the lull to strengthen their new defensive positions along the banks of the river Moselle, 15 miles west of where the men of Loyton were operating. On 5 September the US Third Army relaunched an advance east, liberating the city of Nancy ten days later, but the Germans had been bolstered by the arrival of the Fifth Panzer Division from Brussels and the Allied advance became painstakingly slow.

'The people, who had expected to welcome American soldiers in a matter of days, had to wait now for nearly three months,' remarked Sykes. 'We, the English troops, were faced with a new problem: we had to find an area free from "the grey lice" (as the Germans were called) where we could receive our armed transport and equipment, and then attack.'

In the confusion of their arrival, Franks and Druce had became separated and it was another 48 hours before they had the chance to discuss the situation in any depth. In the interim Franks had had the opportunity to meet Colonel Jean Maximum, the Maquis leader, who 'was not particularly pleased to see me'. For his part Franks was dismayed to learn that all the containers that had been dropped with his party had been stripped bare save for the plastic explosive (minus the chunk eaten by a ravenous Russian) and ammunition.

On 3 September Franks, Maximum and Druce held a conference on future operations, but their best-laid plans were thrown into disarray the following day as Franks and Skyes were reconnoitring the town of Baccarat, 15 miles west of Moussey. 'During that afternoon we heard considerable small arms fire from about a kilometre away from the direction of Veney,' commented Franks. 'We heard later that the Maquis had destroyed an enemy lorry with eight Germans. Shortly afterwards the French were attacked by a large force and surrounded. About 250 French were killed.'

Christopher Sykes (*right*) was not a guerrilla fighter but as a French-speaking liaison officer he was invaluable in the Vosges.

This meant that the area was too compromised for Franks and the next day Druce set off to scout for a new base. He was hindered by a lack of transport but eventually he returned saying that Pierre-Percée, about 7 miles north-west of Moussey, was suitable and the mayor, Monsieur Michel, had assured him that 'no Germans had been near his village for a month'.

The SAS trekked to their new camp in the early hours of 5 September, and the following evening they received their first resupply, including arms for a hundred men. On the evening of 6/7 September Major Denis Reynolds and eleven men parachuted onto the DZ. There should have been more reinforcements but three of Reynolds' stick – Sergeant Michael Fitzpatrick, and Privates John Conway and John Elliott – had vanished in the ground mist that rolled in just as the soldiers jumped. A second aircraft containing more men under the command of Captain Scott returned to England having failed to identify the DZ lights. A few days later Franks heard a rumour that three English soldiers, one of whom had both legs broken, had been discovered by Germans hidden in a house in Pexonne, a couple of miles west of the DZ.

The SAS moved to a new base on 10 September near the town of Celles but the next day a thirty-strong German patrol was seen approaching. Franks had established a Bren gun position on this route but to his horror the Frenchmen who were supposed to be manning the post had wandered off. 'The enemy, although only 5–10 yards from my position, were hidden by trees, and we were unable to open fire,' commented Franks. 'It is not clear as to whether the enemy knew for certain that we were there or not, but they fired into the bushes unpleasantly close. I sent Lieut. Black and his stick to cut them off and ambush them down the path but unfortunately Lieut. Black was not sufficiently quick in obeying my order to catch them in time.'

Druce was in his element in the Vosges. He had taken to donning civilian clothes and wandering into villages and towns to observe the Germans. Other SAS soldiers were struggling with the claustrophobic nature of their existence. 'Pressure affects men in different ways,' reflected Druce. 'The second in command, Dennis Reynolds, was really supposed to take on my job but he just wasn't at home ... he was unsuited to the environment.' Reynolds was a neophyte to this sort of warfare and may not have appreciated its danger. Not long after landing he requested that his black retriever dog be dropped on the next resupply. The request was not fulfilled.

In his report on Loyton, Franks was brutally candid about the quality of some of the soldiers on the operation, particularly those who were inserted later. 'Some of the men sent with the jeeps as final reinforcements were quite unsuitable,' he wrote. 'They arrived very nervous, and were either so scared as to be useless or so confident that they were extremely careless. Most of these men were recent recruits who were clearly not of the right type and had not had sufficient training. This operation showed very clearly that both officers and men who had not had previous battle experience were very nervous, and inclined to spread this disease amongst others. The experienced men were good and could almost always be guaranteed to get away with it.'

In contrast, one of the best soldiers was Corporal Len Owens, a Phantom signaller who parachuted into the Vosges with Franks. A Liverpudlian, the 23-year-old had served in North Africa and Sicily before volunteering for special forces and his reliability during Loyton 'won the admiration and respect of all ranks', as the citation for his Military Medal stated.

Len Owens (*front row, middle*), pictured in Egypt in 1943, was a skilled and reliable signaller.

Another redoubtable figure was Lew Fiddick, the shot-down Canadian airman, who adapted effortlessly to life as a guerrilla fighter. 'Having grown up on Vancouver Island the forest was an environment in which I felt comfortable,' he said. 'I took to the SAS type of warfare quite quickly and it was interesting work.' Fiddick was an important asset to Druce, as was his sergeant, Jock Hay, and the three of them formed a close-knit team. Fiddick even persuaded Hay to consider the idea of emigrating to Vancouver Island after the war.

Druce recalled that it was the drip-drip-drip of tension that gradually wore down some men. 'Every day was a struggle of some sort because of lack of supplies, lack of food, the discomfort of always being in wet clothes,' he reflected. 'And there was no question of finding a place where you could relax in any form.'

The SAS relocated once more, this time to the head of a gully, north-east of Moussey. Yet another impediment to their ability to operate was encountered on 13 September: the weather, with dense cloud making it impossible to receive a much-needed resupply. It was now early autumn and the Vosges was becoming more inhospitable by the day, with the Nazis and the weather combining to hem in the British. To add to Franks' woes, Major Reynolds, Captain Whatley-Smith and Lieutenant Black were all missing.

Finally on the night of 14/15 September a resupply was effected and, in another fillip, Lieutenant Colonel Franks made the acquaintance of a new Maquis group commanded by Colonel Marlier, who 'were first-class'. They were responsible for locating Major Power's stick and reuniting the two units.

Despite the problems, Operation Loyton had enjoyed some success. Lieutenant Rudolf Marx – whose nickname in the regiment predictably was 'Karl' – had spent a week sabotaging enemy traffic on the Celles to Brouville road, destroying at least three vehicles, although three of his nine men – Sergeant Frank Terry-Hall, Corporal Iveson and Private Crozier were missing after they became separated during a firefight with a Nazi patrol in the village of La Chapellotte.

Franks took possession of eighteen containers on the night of 15/16 September but he was appalled to discover that there were no tyre bursters or grenades 'which I had particularly requested'.

Incidentally, on this same night another 2SAS operation, codenamed Pistol, was activated, with three sticks (a fourth returned to Britain having failed to identify the DZ) inserted to the north of Loyton between the cities of Metz and Nancy with instructions to disrupt rail links. We will not concern ourselves with this operation as it was of little consequence, although not for want of trying on the part of its participants. Poorly planned and poorly supplied with food and explosives, the men of Pistol had no Maquis support and achieved very little.

Back at Loyton, bad weather forced the cancellation of two resupplies on the nights of the 18th and 19th but on the evening of the 20th six men, nine containers and, best of all, three jeeps arrived by parachute. Two nights later three more jeeps descended from the sky, along with fourteen men, including the experienced Captain Bridges MacGibbon-Lewis and Lieutenant Jim Silly, who had taken part in Operation Trueform the previous month.

The arrival of the jeeps opened a new vista for the SAS, and with Franks having recently received a signal to the effect that the Americans should reach their area any day, it was decided to launch offensive patrols immediately. Captain Miller and Lieutenant Silly were sent out on foot to attack Germans on the Senones to Moyenmoutier road, while Franks organised six jeep crews, all of three men, except his own, which was four strong to accommodate Captain Sykes. The respective jeep commanders were Druce, Power, MacGibbon-Lewis, Lieutenant David Dill, a member of the advance party of 13 August, who had proved a very capable officer, and Lord John Manners, who had inserted into Loyton fresh from Operation Wallace.

At 1700 hours on 22 September the six jeeps set off in convoy, travelling through Moussey and laagering for the night in the woods near Celles. At dawn the next day Druce and Manners were off 'hunting' in their jeeps, positioning themselves on the Senones to Moyenmoutier road. Druce had no joy for several hours, and he and Sergeant Hay, his front gunner, and his Russian private called Boris Kasperovitch (who served as 'Boris King' and

David Dill (*far left*) and James Black (*far right*) are among the 2SAS officers enjoying the Scottish scenery in 1944. Neither survived Loyton.

joined the regiment from 362 Alien Pioneer Corps), in the rear, were feeling it was not going to be their day. Then they heard the sound of a vehicle. The SAS opened fire as soon as it hove into view. 'Unfortunately it turned out to be our very friendly mayor from Moussey,' recalled Druce. Bullets ripped through the decrepit electric brougham, as Jules Py jumped for his life into a ditch. 'I'm damned if I know how he got out of there,' said Druce. 'But he later sent me and Brian two bottles of champagne, with a little note attached – *"Merci pour le salve tire en mon honneur ce matin"* [Thank you for the salvo fired in my honour this morning].'

Mayor Jules Py, who celebrated his narrow escape from an SAS ambush by sending them two bottles of champagne.

Meanwhile Franks led the other four jeeps on a reconnaissance of the Celles valley and en route stopped at a farm he knew to be friendly in the hope of obtaining information. Power and MacGibbon-Lewis carried on looking for targets, and soon found one – a large convoy. The SAS opened fire, shooting up three staff cars and a lorry packed with troops.

Franks and Dill then headed across country to Allarmont but the enemy was out in force and they were spotted by a bicycle patrol. 'We found a grassy bank on which we waited with both jeeps,' wrote Franks in his report. 'Shortly after getting into position, a German on a bicycle came slowly towards us and we heard men debussing from transport round both corners. We had been unable to test our guns so I decided to fire at the cyclist, who presumably was killed. We were then fired on from a house on the opposite side of the road which was apparently occupied by Germans. Both jeeps gave the house several bursts and then started to make towards the track; in doing so the rear wheels of my jeep slipped and the jeep overturned. I was obliged to abandon it and went up the track on the bonnet of Lieut. Dill's jeep. After travelling some 800 yards the track was found to be blocked by some tree trunks. As infantry were now deployed on both sides of the track and coming towards us, we were obliged to abandon the second jeep and eventually made good our escape.'

Enraged by the guerrilla attacks, the Germans descended on Moussey early the next morning, 24 September, and ordered all the men to assemble in front of the village school. Christopher Sykes was told later what happened next. 'The Gestapo commandant harangued them,' he recounted. 'He said that the Germans knew that there were parachutists in the region, that the most severe punishment was in consequence to be meted out to the men of the town as a warning to other French towns and as a retribution on this community.' The

Nazi paused and then said: 'But we will allow one generous exception. If any man will come forward now with information about the parachutists he will be given his liberty.'

Several of the villagers shivering in the cold knew the whereabouts of the Maquis and SAS camps but they said nothing. In total, 220 male inhabitants of Moussey were rounded up and taken away. Only seventy returned at the end of the war. Henri Poirson was one of them, having survived a brief spell at Auschwitz – where, as a young, fit man, his task was to collect the dead each morning in a barrow – and then Dachau.

The news of the mass arrests dampened the spirits of the SAS. The weather also lowered their mood. 'It had now been raining continuously for four days and was bitterly cold,' wrote Franks. 'I found morale at the base low, and therefore decided to disperse temporarily and billet as many men as I could at houses in the area.'

Druce was unaffected by events and on 25 September he returned to HQ having 'had some good shoots at Germans in La Petite Raon, Le Puid, Le Vermont and Moussey'. He had arrived in Moussey not long after the round-up of the male villagers, and there was still a sizeable number of Nazis around. 'The German commander of an SS unit was just assembling his men when we appeared,' recalled Druce. 'I wasn't expecting to see them but then they didn't expect to see me.' Druce pressed his foot to the floor and accelerated towards the Nazis. 'We opened fire with the Vickers from about 40 yards … and fired off two or three pans of ammunition and took off into the mountains.' In his report, Franks remarked that Druce had expended 400 rounds at close range and there was a 'minimum killed 15/20'.

Druce had taken great satisfaction in killing the SS because of the respect in which he held the French civilians. 'I had more contact with the villagers than anyone because I would go down to the village and talk to them,' he explained. 'I never met anyone in the village – but one – who was anything but supremely kind and helpful.' In particular, Druce admired the women, most of whom were as trustworthy as they were fearless.

Major Power also returned to base with some good news, in his case the order of battle of the 21st Panzer Division, while the ever-reliable Jim Silly had contrived to blow up two staff cars and a 3-ton truck using 'home-made mines of plastic and fog signals'.

So important did Franks consider Power's intelligence that he ordered Druce and Fiddick to make their way through the Nazi lines to the Americans, where he was to deliver the order of battle of the 21st Panzer Division and then return with some new crystals for their malfunctioning radio. 'We didn't have too much trouble getting out,' said Druce. It took two days and the only moment of tension was when they crossed a river, slipping past two guards on the bridge.

Lew Fiddick (*left*) with Harry Doe and Al Peabody in June 1944. All three baled out of their Lancaster but only Fiddick avoided capture and death.

In the week after Druce and Fiddick exfiltrated, the net began to tighten on A Squadron, 2SAS. There were skirmishes with Germans and confused reports of SAS soldiers in the hands of the enemy. Colonel Jean Maximum, the Maquis leader, was as truculent and as timid as ever, informing Franks that 'his Maquis had no intention of operating until after the arrival of the Americans in the area'.

On 7 October MacGibbon-Lewis returned from a recce to report that the area was 'full of enemy, food short and the French too frightened to help'. Two days later, with their supplies of rations and explosives dwindling, and the likelihood of a successful resupply remote due to the presence of the enemy, Franks 'decided to end the operation and instruct parties to make their way to the American lines as best they could'. He issued coordinates for a rendezvous (a deserted house) where he, Power, Skyes, his sergeant-major and two of the Phantom team, Captain John Hislop and Corporal Len Owens, would remain for 48 hours. Franks then detailed six men to wait for an overdue sabotage party to return before guiding them through the lines; the half dozen were handpicked by the lieutenant colonel, his most doughty men, led by David Dill and including Druce's sergeant, Jock Hay.

Franks' party reached the American lines without incident but others of 2SAS were not so fortunate. Captain MacGibbon-Lewis and nine men set off from a sawmill on 9 October, heading north-west across the Celles road and then turning west once they were in thick forest. The next day they reached the expansive river Meurthe close to the village of Baccarat. MacGibbon-Lewis and two men stripped and swam across the river but it was a struggle. The water was cold and the current, given the incessant rain of recent weeks, was strong. Only Lieutenant Manners had the confidence in his swimming ability to ford the river, which he did, but the rest, under the command of Lieutenant Jim Silly, decided to find a bridge. After several hours of fruitless searching, the six men returned to the river bank from where their comrades had swum across. They had no option other than to swim the river.

'As we undressed to swim across I became aware that Jock Robb was doing nothing,' recalled Dusty Crossfield. 'He then told me that he was staying where he was because he couldn't swim. He'd lied during training and got through somehow without being found out. It was too difficult a crossing for me to ferry him over and I was damned if I was going to leave a good pal so I got dressed again and we decided to find our own way by a different route back to safety.'

Lieutenant Silly and the other three men got safely across and continued their trek towards the Allied lines. However, about 5 miles west of the river Meurthe, close to the village of Menarmont, they encountered a German patrol. There was an exchange of fire and the SAS scattered, Silly and 18-year-old Private Donald Lewis going one way, and Corporal Larley and Private Herbert going another. A bullet caught Herbert in the buttocks but with the help of Larley they evaded the Germans.

It was now bitterly cold and Herbert was exhibiting the first signs of exposure. Larley left his comrade in the woods on the night of 12/13 October and set off towards the village of St Pierremont in the hope of finding a barn in which to lie up. 'In the village I was challenged by a French sentry, whom I thought at first to be a Milice,' recounted Larley. 'After some talk he turned out to be from a forward platoon of the 2nd French Division.'

Crossfield and Robb also made it safely to Allied lines, thanks to the courage and hospitality of a Frenchman, who sheltered the pair in his house in Baccarat for three days. Then the Germans arrived. They were taking over the village as a defensive fortification and all the civilians were given 36 hours to evacuate. Their host put Crossfield and Robb in contact with the Maquis and two young Frenchmen escorted the British soldiers towards an isolated bridge. But they were challenged by a German patrol en route and, taking to their heels, they knew they would have to cross the Meurthe by swimming. 'I told Jock to place his hands on my shoulders once we were in the water,' recalled Crossfield. 'He looked very undecided. I said it was either that or stay and get shot.'

The pair got across, wet and cold but relieved, and pressed on through the woods until they reached American lines. Once their identity had been established, Crossfield and Robb were driven north to Lunéville. 'Arriving at the barracks we were greeted by Colonel Franks,' remembered Crossfield.

'Captains Hislop and [MacGibbon-]Lewis were also there and informed us that we were just in time to go back to Blighty for a spot of leave. Corporal Larley had arrived safely back and was on his way to Paris for some leave, but many of the boys never did make it.'

Among those who failed to appear were Lieutenants Jim Silly and David Dill, Captain Victor Gough, and Sergeant Jock Hay. They had vanished.

*   *   *

On 6 May 1946 the trial began in Wuppertal of several men complicit to some degree in the murder of twenty-nine* members of 2SAS. Among those in the dock were Colonel Erich Isselhorst, the Gestapo commander in Alsace, SS General Carl Oberg, the Gestapo chief for France, and Colonel Wilhelm Schneider, the Gestapo chief in Strasbourg. Major Alastair Hunt, prosecuting counsel, said in his opening address: 'The simplicity of the facts of the case are equalled only by the cold-blooded ferocity with which the crime was carried out.'

Major Hunt, a solicitor in civilian life, had been due for demobilisation at the beginning of 1946, but he was so disturbed by the case that 'he felt it his duty to remain in the service until all those involved in the murders had been brought to justice'.

The accused were in court thanks to what one British newspaper called the 'tireless search' by Major Eric Barkworth, Intelligence Officer of 2SAS, and an equally dedicated team of nineteen SAS personnel, who left no stone unturned in their quest to find those responsible for the murder of their comrades. They had scoured the British, French and American zones of Germany for the guilty, following up leads gleaned from witnesses of many nationalities.

Captain Yurka Galitzine, an Anglo-Russian, who was working for an Allied unit investigating German atrocities in the Occupied countries, saw how Barkworth also deployed cunning to catch his prey. 'He heard that one of the key people wanted was in the Russian zone, near Leipzig, and so he impersonated the Gestapo chief [Wilhelm Schneider] on the telephone – the telephone system was still working in those days, through the various zones – and he said to this Gestapo man: 'I'm on to a frightfully good thing on the black market. If you meet me under the clock in Cologne railway station on such-and-such a day, at midnight, I'll cut you in on it and we can share the proceeds together.' And this fellow fell for it, the SAS team were waiting in the shadows and they grabbed the prisoner.'

---

* Thirty-four men were killed during Operation Loyton and it is believed twenty-nine of them were murdered. Of the other five, four were killed in combat – Robert Lodge, George Johnston, Peter Bannerman and Maurice Boissarie – and one, Boris Kasperovitch, was accidentally shot dead when he answered a password in Russian.

Eric Barkworth led the SAS investigation in the murder of their comrades with a fierce determination.

The SAS war crimes team brought many of those responsible for the Loyton murders to justice.

In his report on the case, Barkworth had prefaced his findings with a quote from *Macbeth*, Act 1, Scene VII:

> But in these cases
> We still have judgement here; that we but teach
> Bloody instructions, which being taught return
> To plague the inventor.

The trial lasted for two months, during which time the court heard what had happened to the twenty-nine 2SAS soldiers who had been captured during Operation Loyton. Only one was alive, Sergeant Ken Seymour, the Jedburgh wireless operator, who was the first to fall into enemy hands. Ginger Hall, Dusty Crossfield's friend, was caught a short while later having been wounded in the firefight in the woods. The 23-year-old Londoner was taken to a camp at Schirmeck on the edge of the town of the same name, 30 miles west of Strasbourg. Constructed in 1940, Schirmeck camp could hold up to 1,500 prisoners and its commandant was a First World War veteran called Karl Buck, described as a 'neat white-haired little man'.

Hall's body was the only one of the dead SAS men not to have been found. Wilhelm Schneider told the court he remembered Hall because of his fair hair and fresh complexion. He insisted he had nothing to do with his death, telling the court that Buck's driver had informed him that the Englishman was shot by a country road as he was being driven the 6 miles south from Schirmeck to the concentration camp at Natzweiler-Struthof. It is believed Hall was thrown into the camp's incinerator.

There was less uncertainty about the fate of Sergeant Gerald Davis, the Phantom signaller, who became separated from his comrades during the ambush on 17 August. For three days the former railway employee from Maidenhead sheltered in the woods, emerging from his hideout early on a Sunday morning. He sought help from the villagers of Saint-Jean le Saulcy, but a farmer refused to give him food and shelter, as did the village priest, Abbé Colin. But he did say he would fetch help from the Maquis. Instead the priest hurried over to the Belval château and betrayed Davis to the Kommando Schöner.

Later that day Davis was taken to Schirmeck and handed to Wilhelm Schneider for interrogation. The Nazi had already gleaned much information from the cooperative Sergeant Seymour, but Davis was an altogether different proposition. John Hislop had worked with Davis for more than a year in Phantom and admired his physical and mental qualities. 'He was a tall, lean, athletically built young man, intelligent, responsible and absolutely reliable,' he remembered. The auburn-haired Davis was as obsessed with cricket as Hislop was with horse racing, and the pair frequently tried to convert the other to their particular sport. Above all, recalled Hislop, Davis was 'not over-awed by anyone'. He was his own man, and when asked he aired his opinions

Justice was not served in the case of Karl Buck, who served just two years' imprisonment for his part in the Loyton atrocities.

candidly. On one occasion Davis's commanding officer had come across Davis leaning against his broken-down scout car. 'Why are you standing about doing fuck all?' demanded the officer. Davis shrugged and replied: 'Cos there's fuck all to do.'

Face to face with Davis, Schneider asked him to pinpoint on a map the whereabouts of the SAS camps. Davis said nothing. He was struck about the neck and shoulder but still he remained silent. Unable to extract anything from his prisoner, Schneider told Davis he had 'ten minutes to make up his mind': either talk or die. Schneider left Davis alone and returned when the time was up. He 'refused to talk'. Schneider shrugged: 'You know what happens to terrorists.'

Davis was given a final chance. He was driven back into the forest, not far from the spot where the Nazis and the SAS had exchanged fire on 17 August. Lead us to your hideout or we will shoot you, he was told. Davis said nothing.

On 1 April 1945, Easter Sunday, Albert Freine, a forest ranger based at Moussey, discovered a badly decomposed body in woods near Jardin David. There was a bullet hole in the skull and he was 'wearing khaki trousers with an exterior bellows pocket, English boots and braces'. The next day a mass was held for the unknown soldier in the church at Moussey and afterwards he was laid to rest in the adjacent cemetery. In July the corpse was exhumed and examined by Barkworth's team. He signalled his initial thoughts to SAS HQ: 'Excessive zeal French extracted teeth from upper jaw. Those handed over loose with hair ... [will] refit teeth sockets and check. Hair unusual. Colour auburn.' Two days later, on 4 July, Barkworth sent a second signal, detailing the result of a dental examination on the skull's teeth. He concluded: 'Consider [this] with evidence hair and map ref[erence] where found adequate proof Davis.'

Another mystery solved during the trial concerned the disappearance of Sergeant Michael Fitzpatrick and Privates John Conway and John Elliott, who had failed to reach the DZ on the evening of 6/7 September when Major Denis Reynolds inserted. Like Davis, their misfortune had been to encounter a duplicitous local. Elliott, who was from Manchester, had broken his thigh on landing and his two comrades had remained with him. Fitzpatrick was a seasoned soldier, one of the original commandos, who had been awarded a Military Medal in December 1941 for his gallantry during operations against the enemy at Vaagso and Maaloy. He had joined 2SAS in May 1943, one of the first when the regiment was raised by Bill Stirling. Conway was only 19.

The three had taken shelter in a remote farm, known as La Fosse, on the western side of Lake Pierre-Percée. For more than a week they were looked after by the farm's occupants, the widowed Delphine Jacquot, 69, and her son Lucien. Word, however, of the soldiers' presence leaked out and reached the ears of two sisters, Geneviève Demetz, 16 and her sister Yvette, who was a year younger. Their mother had died when they were younger and they lived with their layabout father. To escape their troubled home life they took jobs at the German military hospital at Baccarat and over time came to the attention of the Milice. Although they were too young to join the fascist paramilitary unit, the sisters enjoyed the power and status that came with the much-feared unit and they did odd jobs for the Milice in the summer of 1944.

Initially the Maquis considered the girls as harmless irritants but then they began to wonder if they weren't Nazi informants. On the night of

24/25 August the Maquis abducted the sisters and brought them to the camp they shared with the SAS. 'They were arrogant and dirty,' recalled one of the Maquis, René Ricatte, whose alias was Lieutenant Jean Serge. 'First and foremost, Henry [Druce] told me to shave their hair, a task incidentally that was so unappealing that he did it himself, before Marc interrogated them.' Once that was done, the French started to argue among themselves as to what to do with the girls. The majority view was that they should be shot. Druce suggested 'turning them over to French justice' when, as expected, the advance elements of Leclerc's Second Armoured Division arrived in the area in a few days.

Dusty Crossfield recalled the events many years later in an article for *Mars & Minerva*, the regimental journal of the SAS. 'Their captors wanted to shoot them on the spot but our officers were not having any of that so a compromise was reached and their hair was shaved off, and they were set to work on camp duties.' This statement conflicts a little with what René Ricatte stated, when he implied that he and the Frenchmen were reluctant to shave the girls' hair so Druce took it upon himself to wield the scissors. It might have been the case that the Maquis told Druce he had to perform the onerous task if he had denied them the opportunity of killing two people they considered traitors.

Many of the British SAS soldiers witnessed similar acts of vengeance during their time in France, and while nearly all found it distasteful, few passed judgement. Harry Vickers, of Operation Wallace, reflected: 'I've often thought about the business of collaboration, and it's easy for us to criticise them but say you're the village electrician or something like that and you're occupied and your electricity isn't working and the Germans tell you to mend it. What can you do? You've got all your fellow citizens to think about, you can't just say oh no. We saw some of the shaved head business and we knew why they were doing it, I just ignored it.'

Henry Druce mentioned the incident of the girls in his operational report, describing the Demetz sisters as 'Milicien prostitutes'. He added: '[They] were brought to the camp, where they were kept by the French under lax guard. It was a foolish action to bring them near the camp for after they escaped it became dangerous for anyone in civilian clothes, because the two girls went round towns and villages with the Germans, denouncing anyone who had been with the Maquis.'

The sisters had been put to work in the Maquis kitchen but they escaped a fortnight later when a German patrol strayed close to the camp and distracted their guards. Taken to the Gestapo HQ at the Hotel du Pont in Baccarat, Geneviève and Yvette told the Nazis everything they could about their captors. It was Geneviève who tipped off the Germans about the three SAS soldiers sheltering at the Farm Fosse. How she knew they were there is not known, but on 16 September she guided a detachment of Nazis from the Kommando Wenger to the isolated hideout.

Madame Jacquot and her son were summarily executed by the Nazis. Fitzpatrick, Conway and Elliot were bundled into a truck and taken to a house at La Neuveville, approximately 20 miles south-west of La Fosse. There they were held for three days, during which time Yvette Demetz brought them food. She saw them taken from the house on 19 September. The soldiers were driven back to La Fosse by two Germans and four Milice and herded inside a small stone barn. They had probably guessed their fate long before they were machine-gunned. On leaving, the Nazis set fire to the barn.

At her trial in May 1946, Yvette Demetz told the court of another SAS man to whom she served food while he was a prisoner, a soldier she recognised from a photograph as Lieutenant Jim Silly. He was held in the cellar of the Ecole du Vivier at Étival-Clairefontaine, along with some Frenchman, one of whom was Maurice Simon, who was subsequently released. Silly appeared to understand that he was unlikely to see England again; he wrote his address on a scrap of paper and handed it to Simon. The paper had later been confiscated by the Nazis but Simon was able to recall part of the address: 'Greenvay'. Silly's parents lived at Greenway, Berkhamstead.

Silly and the Frenchmen, who were accused of being Maquisards, were subjected to several days of torture. Then, aware that the Allies were approaching from the west, the Nazis loaded the fourteen prisoners into a lorry in the afternoon of 22 October and drove a few miles into the forest. Living rough in the trees there was a Maquisard who had escaped from German custody a few days earlier. He watched a lorry containing numerous men and an accompanying Nazi staff car drive in the direction of an isolated sawmill. He lost sight of them but a short while later heard 'a deafening noise of a long burst of firing'. When the vehicles reappeared there were no men on the lorry.

As was their custom, the Germans attempted to conceal their butchery by burning the evidence and when French investigators visited the scene they had to remove a great deal of rubble to find what was underneath. There were few distinguishing marks left on the charred corpses but Dr Thomassin, the doctor of the nearby town of Moyenmoutier, did find 'a pair of steel-rimmed spectacles, and a spectacle case off which the leather had been burnt'.

Major Barkworth had the names of the thirteen Frenchmen held in the cellar with Silly. After making some enquiries he established that only the Englishman had worn spectacles.

The Demetz sisters made up in cunning what they lacked in morality and evaded justice for many more months despite an extensive search. Eventually they were arrested in July 1945 and imprisoned in Nancy, but they soon escaped and were caught a few weeks later. In May 1946 they were convicted of providing intelligence to the enemy and Geneviève was sentenced to life in prison with forced labour. Her younger sister received twenty years. Both were condemned to '*dégradation nationale*' for life; this was a sentence handed down to the most serious cases of treachery and included the forfeiture of the right to vote and a ban on working in the civil service or in any position of authority in the media. It is not known what became of the sisters upon their release.

There was a grim litany of other testimonies told to the court throughout the early summer of 1946, of SAS soldiers murdered singly or in pairs, or on occasion in groups of eight.

On Thursday, 13 July the court gave judgment on the accused. While the verdicts were being considered, Colonel Erich Isselhorst approached the chief interpreter, Major Robert Forrest, saying 'I thank you for your good work. Please could you give me a cigarette before I hear the verdict?' Forrest removed a case from his tunic pocket and gave the German a cigarette.

The *Dundee Courier* was one of several British newspapers that reported the verdict the following day:

> A British parachute officer's tireless search still continuing – for the murderers of 29 of his comrades resulted at Wuppertal, Germany, yesterday in death sentences on three German officers and prison sentences on two others. A sixth was found not guilty. The British officer is Major E.A. Barkworth, intelligence officer of the Special Air Service, whose search began when he found a mass grave. The Germans he brought to trial were Colonel Isselhorst, Gestapo commander in Alsace; SS General Oberg, Gestapo chief for France; and Colonel Schneider, Gestapo chief in Strasbourg – all sentenced to hang … all were accused of being involved in the killing of British and French parachutists in the Vosges mountains in October 1944. They pleaded that the parachutists broke the laws of war by collaborating with the Maquis. Some of the parachutists were shot, others hanged and cremated.'

Len Owens cut out the report on the verdict from the *Daily Mirror*, and sent it to his fiancée, having underlined Isselhorst's name. Along the top of the cutting, Owens wrote: 'This is what all the flap was about a few weeks ago. The chap with name underlined should be given a slow death. I'm glad to have had a hand in his death even though it will be quick.'

Schneider was executed by the British in January 1947. Oberg and Isselhorst were handed to the French, who wanted to put both men on trial for crimes committed against French nationals. In April 1947 Isselhorst escaped from captivity and for two weeks a huge manhunt ensued. He was recaptured and put on trial by the French. Found guilty, Isselhorst was executed in Strasbourg in February 1948.

Oberg, dubbed 'The Butcher of Paris', was sentenced to a similar fate but he appealed and instead of facing a firing squad, he was given a life sentence. In November 1962 he was released after a pardon from President Charles de Gaulle, as part of the Franco-German partnership that had been growing since the establishment in 1957 of the European Economic Community.

Henry Druce received a DSO for his role in Operation Loyton (see Appendix III) but he was despondent that his attempts to have two of his dead comrades recognised for their courage and fortitude came to naught. 'Neither David Dill nor Jock Hay were sufficiently rewarded by the award of only a Mention in Despatches,' he said in an interview in 2003. 'There is no such thing as justice in this world.'

What to visit on Operation Loyton

Le Mont DZ

With so many sites of interest to visit, Operation Loyton presents one of the most far-ranging pilgrimages of any SAS mission in Occupied France. We shall start where it all began in the early hours of 13 August 1944, on the DZ where Captain Henry Druce and his advance party landed. Naturally, it's a very remote spot, and the nearest village is Le Mont, approximately 1½ miles south of Moussey. If you approach the village on the D49, via Le Saulcy, you come into Le Mont on the Rue Principale and then at a fork (**GPS 48.408826, 7.026519**) turn off down the unnamed lane on the right (by a wooden bus shelter) and continue for nearly half a mile as the lane curves to the left until it debouches into a meadow (**GPS 48.408890, 7.017552**). The French christened the DZ 'Anatomy' because of a coded message broadcast on the BBC 'From Manicoco to Bamboula, the priest Pellerin will visit this evening the anatomy of Bamboula'.

This DZ was also the site of a massive resupply of arms for the FFI on the night of 6/7 September. According to Druce, they trekked for eight hours on foot in the company of the Maquis to their camp, known as 'A'.

Le Mont DZ, codenamed 'Anatomy', where the Loyton advance party landed on 13 August.

Camp A

Situated on the top of Col des Marcassins (**GPS 48.474946, 7.037168**) deep in the forest, 5 miles north of Moussey, Camp A had a commanding view of the countryside. 'The base was a very large log cabin in a cleared area almost on top of a peak,' recalled Ronald 'Dusty' Crossfield.

One of the forest tracks on the Col des Marcassins in 2021. Close to this spot the SAS engaged a German patrol on 17 August.

The col, which is signposted, is accessible by some well-maintained tracks and it is possible to drive in a suitable vehicle most of the way. If you decide to ascend on foot, wear the right footwear and clothing, because while the route is fairly easy, the col is at an altitude of 2,250ft and the weather in this region is temperamental.

The Château of Belval

In walking from Camp A to Camp B you are following in the approximate footsteps of Druce and his men on the afternoon of 17 August 1944. According to Sergeant Ken Seymour: 'We were proceeding along a narrow mountain path, single file. I was about half way down the column ... firing started but from my position in the column I could not discover what was going on. The column left the path and endeavoured to scatter to the undergrowth.'

Seymour, the only member of 2SAS who survived captivity (see Chapter 5), claimed in a post-operational report that he valiantly fought off the Germans for a considerable time, first with his Bren gun, then with a carbine and finally with his revolver. Having expended all his ammunition, Seymour had the presence of mind to 'dive into a sort of cave mouth and destroy my papers, wireless plan and [radio] crystals by burning them'. He was then surrounded by about fifteen Germans who took him prisoner.

This contradicts the findings of Major Barkworth, who was told by the Maquis that Seymour was being carried on a stretcher along the mountain path because of his toe injury. Why would he therefore have been entrusted with the Bren, as well as carrying his own carbine? Seymour had joined the Royal Armoured Corps as a wireless operator; he was not a trained infantry-man and it is fanciful in the extreme to imagine him, in his first contact with the enemy, putting up such a staunch fight, and all while carrying a wound that had immobilised him since landing four days earlier.

During his trial Wilhelm Schneider said that Seymour was very angry at having been abandoned, the inference being that the men carrying his stretcher ran off into the undergrowth when the firing started.

Once in captivity, Seymour was taken to the Château at Belval (**GPS 48.410129, 7.044845**), approximately 2 miles south-east of Moussey. Completed in 1904 by the wealthy industrialist Louis-François Nansé, the château (which is in private hands) has changed little in the last three-quarters of a century; austere, angular and sombre, it was a fitting billet for the Nazi Kommando unit that arrived on 16 August. Seymour recalled that he was interrogated at the château by an SS officer who 'spoke excellent English with an American accent'. He was detained that night in the château but in the early hours of 18 August Seymour was driven to Schirmeck camp.

Schirmeck Camp

It is 13 miles from the château at Belval to the camp at Schirmeck where Seymour was taken in a side-car combination on 18 August. As he entered the camp, he would have seen fourteen barracks. Of the fourteen one was a kitchen, another a hospital, and barracks 12, 13 and 14 (which were made of stone) housed female prisoners. The rest contained male prisoners. Seymour said that on arrival he was 'placed on a chair just inside the concentration camp' [*sic*: in fact, it wasn't a concentration camp] and several hours later he was taken off for questioning. During his trial Schneider confirmed that Seymour was made to sit outside the canteen for a long period, during which time he was 'shouted at' by a doctor from Natzweiler-Struthof concentration camp.

At one point the wounded Ginger Hall was brought to the camp. He was also made to sit outside the canteen, just 6 metres from Seymour. Schneider expressed his surprise to the court that during Seymour's testimony to the court he omitted this important detail.

Seymour was detained briefly in the men's cells at Schirmeck, during which time, according to Schneider, he 'was not reluctant to give information'. He received no ill-treatment as a consequence. In the late afternoon of 18 August Seymour was taken under guard from the camp and put on a train at Schirmeck station bound for Strasbourg. He was then sent to Stalag VIIIC in Lower Silesia, and when that was evacuated in February 1945 it is believed Seymour was transferred to Dulag Luft, near Frankfurt.

Barely anything remains today in Schirmeck of the camp, through which around 15,000 prisoners passed between 13 July 1940 and 23 November 1944. Estimates of how many died within the compound vary from seventy-eight – the official Nazi figure – to the French number of 500.

The entrance gate (**GPS 48.478502, 7.218598**) to the town's media library (médiathèque), which was formerly the town hall, was the entrance gate to the camp when it opened in 1940. Not far away is a small plaque on the front of No. 3 Rue du Souvenir, close to the t-junction with the Rue du Donon (**GPS 48.479651, 7.211202**). It explains that the building was the first Nazi camp in annexed Alsace during the war. More specifically, the house was the billet of the camp commandant, Karl Buck. A decorated veteran of the First World War, Buck lost a leg in an accident in the 1920s while working as an engineer in South America. He and several of his guards at Schirmeck were tried in France in 1953 for war crimes. In a trial that lasted ten days, the court listened to the testimony of parents whose sons were tortured, beaten and executed during the four years of the camp's existence.

Before he was given a death sentence, Buck addressed the court: 'I ask you to consider that all the acts which form the basis of this prosecution are my responsibility, and not that of my fellow-accused who, as soldiers, did nothing but obey my orders. Circumstances forced me to carry out a lofty and difficult task in a war in which Germany had everything at stake. It was life or death for the Fatherland. I would be the last to claim that no fault was committed during the accomplishing of this duty.' He also stated that he 'felt immense pity for those who suffered in the camp'. Buck's death sentence was commuted to life imprisonment but he served just two years before being repatriated to West Germany.

Also worth a visit is the Alsace Moselle Memorial (**GPS 48.486514, 7.220456**) just a mile or so north of Schirmeck town centre. A Franco-German project, aimed at establishing a bond of amity in a hotly disputed historical region, the museum (which opened in 2005) focuses on the Second World War but also delves back into the First World War and the Franco-Prussian war of 1870 in an attempt to explain why the region was the only part of France to be annexed to the Third Reich in 1940.

Natzweiler-Struthof concentration camp

Wally 'Ginger' Hall was not so fortunate as the accommodating Sergeant Seymour. Buck ordered his driver, Kurt Giegling, to drive Hall from Schirmeck to the concentration camp at Natzweiler-Struthof. At some point on the 6-mile journey, Hall, who had been wounded during the contact with the Nazis as Druce's party moved through the mountains from Camp A to Camp B, was executed. Most likely the car pulled over and he was dragged from the vehicle and shot. Brian Stonehouse, a British SOE agent, who was incarcerated at Natzweiler, told Major Barkworth after the war that one day in August 1944 he had seen the body of what he presumed was a British airman carried through the camp. The description he gave of the man's face matched

Natzweiler-Struthof concentration camp. The building on the far right is the crematorium and to the left is the prison block. The dormitories stood where the gravel oblongs are visible.

that of Hall. It is believed that Hall was thrown into the camp's oven. He is commemorated on the panelling of the Bayeux Memorial to the Missing in Normandy, along with 1,807 other Commonwealth soldiers killed in the summer of 1944 who have no known grave.

A similar fate had befallen four female members of SOE the previous month: Vera Leigh, Sonya Olschanezky, Diana Rowden and Andree Borrel. Stonehouse saw the women arrive but that was the only sight he had of them. That evening another SOE agent, Pat O'Leary (his nom de guerre – he was in fact a Belgian called Albert Guérisse), looked out of the window of the camp infirmary from where he could see diagonally to the crematorium. The first person he saw was Dr Werner Rohde, the SS doctor, heading towards the crematorium. 'A few minutes later, maybe ten minutes later, a girl was escorted from the gaol across to the crematorium,' recalled O'Leary. 'And then a signal. The signal of the chimney, which all the prisoners at the camp knew very well. The gust of flame bursting out of the chimney of the crematorium, which meant that the door of the oven of the crematorium had been opened and shut.'

There were three more gusts in the minutes that followed. Dr Rohde, along with another doctor, had administered supposedly lethal injections of phenol to the four SOE agents before burning their bodies. However, according to an eyewitness, the phenol injected into the fourth woman was inadequate and she was semi-conscious as she was pushed into the oven. 'Why?' she was heard to ask. 'For typhus,' Dr Rohde replied. Rohde was executed after the war.

In June 1975 the then Prime Minister of France, Jacques Chirac (who later became president), unveiled a plaque at Natzweiler to honour these women.

The following year Neo-Nazis launched an arson attack on the camp's museum, which had been inaugurated in 1965, and it was four years before it was officially reopened. In 2005 a new wing was opened, the European Centre of Deported Resistance Members, dedicated to the history of the concentration camp. It is housed in a barracks recreated from one of the prisoners' dormitory blocks.

The museum is an important and poignant memorial to the only concentration camp built in France. Visitors cannot but fail to be moved as they walk through the camp's ground, hauntingly unchanged from when Natzweiler was the final destination for an estimated 22,000 of the 52,000 prisoners who passed through the camp's gates. The gas chambers and the site of the first crematorium are at the bottom of the camp, and the plaque unveiled by Chirac is one of several in remembrance of SOE agents, Maquis and other brave men and women who were murdered by the Nazis.

The camp had been opened in May 1941, and was constructed on the site of a winter sports resort – Mount Louise – and was chosen by the Nazis because of its geological properties. In 1940 a team of Nazi geologists had uncovered a

The oven at Natzweiler-Struthof concentration camp.

vein of red granite on Mount Louise, and the inmates were put to work in a quarry to extract the granite. The brutal conditions accounted for many of the camp's deaths, but there was also selective extermination in the gas chambers.

To reach Natzweiler (**GPS 48.454450, 7.252826**) from Schirmeck, follow the D130. The camp is well-signposted and there is plenty of parking.

The Lancaster Memorial

Also murdered at Natzweiler were two Canadian airmen, Pilot Officers Al Peabody and Harry Doe, who were captured after they baled out of their stricken Lancaster bomber on the night of 29 July 1944. Their bodies have never been recovered but in 2016 a Canadian investigation team concluded they were executed at the concentration camp within 48 hours of their capture and then incinerated in the oven. Three of the crew were killed in the initial attack on the Lancaster by a Me110 and two others, Lew Fiddick and George Wishart, baled out. Wishart suffered a serious leg injury on landing and was taken to hospital by the Nazis. This saved his life as the Gestapo evidently overlooked his survival. Fiddick made contact with the Maquis and was handed over to the SAS on 15 August. For six weeks Fiddick participated in operations and such was his effectiveness that he was post-Loyton made an honorary member of the SAS.

In 2019 a memorial was unveiled to the crew of Lancaster L7576 (which was on its 99th mission when it was shot down), close to the site where it came down. It is an original and impressive memorial, consisting of a Lancaster tail fin mounted on three levels of local rock. Close by is an information board in English and in French. The memorial is at GPS 48.53420,6.99347, approximately 20 miles from Natzweiler. Take the D130 from the camp north towards Schirmeck and then head west on the D392.

The church of Saint-Jean-du-Mont, Le Saulcy

On 20 August, three days after Wally Hall and Ken Seymour had been captured, Sergeant Gerald Davis, the Phantom signaller, emerged from the woods and sought help from the villagers of Saulcy. A farmer turned him away and so he went to the church of Saint-Jean-du-Mont in the parish of Le Saulcy (**GPS 48.412827, 7.038032**). The priest, Abbé Colin, deceived Davis into thinking he would help him, but in fact he went to the Belval château and betrayed the Englishman to the Kommando Schöner. It is not known what happened to Abbé Colin after the war.

Lieutenant Colonel Brian Franks DZ

Ten days after the capture of Gerald Davis, the CO of 2SAS, Lieutenant Colonel Brian Franks, parachuted onto a hastily arranged DZ at Neufmaisons. Franks landed just after 0300 hours, and among the reception committee on the DZ was Dusty Crossfield. 'Hello Dusty', he said, 'where are the porters?'

Belval Château, where Sergeant Davies was taken for interrogation after being denounced by the priest of Le Saulcy.

Len Owens at the grave of Gerald Davies in Moussey cemetery in 2005.

I remember thinking 'Christ, this isn't Victoria Station', when a tremendous racket started: one of the canisters had exploded and it was like bloody Guy Fawkes' night.'

There is nothing of any significance on the site of the DZ (**GPS 48.465615, 6.827317**), which is 8 miles west of Le Saulcy.

La Fosse farm

A week after the arrival of Franks and his party, Major Denis Reynolds and another stick of reinforcements inserted on a misty night. Three of the men, Sergeant Michael Fitzpatrick, and Privates John Conway and John Elliott, did not assemble on the DZ on the eastern side of Lake Pierre-Percée. The trio were the last to exit the aircraft and not only did they drift to the west of the DZ, coming down on the other side of the lake, but Elliott broke his leg on landing.

The soldiers were taken under the wing of Delphine Jacquot and her son Lucien, on a farm called La Fosse, and for a week they were well tended. Their whereabouts, however, came to the attention of 16-year-old Geneviève Demetz, possibly through a gossiping local or a Maquis informer, and she led the Germans to the farm. The Jacquots were shot, as were Fitzpatrick, Conway and Elliott, in their case in a farm building that was subsequently set alight.

To reach the site (**GPS 48.473003, 6.866566**) from the village of Neuf-maisons, take the D8 north in the direction of Pexonne and turn right up the

It was here, at La Fosse, where Fitzpatrick, Conway and Elliott were murdered. A plaque on the outside wall honours them and the Jacquots.

The graves of Conway, Fitzpatrick and Elliott at Moussey Cemetery.

Chemin du Pinglier until you reach a t-junction. Turn right along the route marked Moisy for half a mile until you see on your right in the middle of a field the stone ruins of the farm Fosse. This is one of the most evocative memorials of all the SAS operations of 1944, a mute and lonely testament to the horrors of war and the best and worst of human nature. A plaque on the front of the stonework explains in French what happened and lists the dead. At the foot of the plaque it is written: 'In homage to these patriots and to the valiant British fighters.'

The Resistance Memorial
A mile west of the Fosse farm, as the crow flies, is another powerful memorial known as the 'Monument de Resistance'. To reach it, head back on the D8 to Neufmaisons and then travel north on the D168 towards Vacquerville. You will see a sign 'Monument de Resistance' and then on the right there are some farm buildings by the road. Take the track that slopes gently upwards and you will reach the monument (**GPS 48.473478, 6.840636**).

The first thing you see are the ruins of what once was the Viombois Farm. During the German attack on 17 August against the SAS and Maquis as they trekked from Camp A to Camp B, the French lost twenty-five men and much of the arsenal. There followed a reorganisation of the Maquis and a unification of local groups, so that by the start of September there were approximately 832 volunteers, of whom only 150 were armed. It was decided to split the force, one section heading east to the Vosges and the other waging a guerrilla campaign in the forests further west towards the Meurthe river.

Before that happened, however, a large drop of arms and ammunition was arranged through Lieutenant Colonel Brian Franks. The resupply was scheduled for the night of 3/4 September but it was postponed for twenty-four hours because of inclement weather.

The Maquis now had to hide out for a day, no easy task given their size, so they headed to the farm at Viombois, which was isolated and surrounded by woodland that was ideal for bivouacing a large force. On the down side it was in close proximity to a major road used frequently by the Nazis. But it was only for one night.

At 0900 hours on 4 September a German vehicle was spotted by a Maquis sentry detail. The men inside the car were engineers who were en route to fix a damaged telephone cable. The callow Frenchmen, believing their whereabouts had been detected, opened fire and took the terrified Germans prisoner. A couple of hours later six more Germans, carrying a supply of new telephone wires to their comrades, were also captured. This time the shots were heard and a large German patrol was despatched to investigate. At 1400 hours the battle of Viombois began. The fighting raged for the rest of the day and into the night, but the outcome was inevitable, given the overwhelming firepower of the Germans. Fifty-seven French fighters were killed in or around the farm, and a further thirty-four were captured, all of whom were later executed at Natzweiler. The Germans lost 134 men in the battle and a further 182 wounded.

Among the Frenchman killed at the farm was Lieutenant Guy Baraud, whose real name was Maurice Boissarie, part of the Jedburgh 'Jacob' Team that had inserted into the Vosges with Henry Druce's SAS advance party on

The Resistance memorial (*far left*) and (*foreground*) the ruins of Viombois farm, scene of a furious battle between the Nazis and the Maquis.

13 August. He is mentioned on the large information plaque attached to the front of the ruined farmhouse, and the site of his death is marked by another plaque, 30 metres to the right of the farmhouse. There are several other small memorials scattered around the ruins of the farm, including on the left-hand side of the main building a tablet listing the fifty-seven Frenchmen who were killed on this site.

To the left of the farm, across the car park, is a commemorative wall on which are inscribed the names of the Maquisards, SOE and British SAS who lost their lives during the fighting in Alsace. Next to it is the granite memorial with a large Cross of Lorraine at its base.

The killing of Lewis and Brown at Le Harcholet

On 9 October Captain MacGibbon-Lewis and nine men set off from a saw-mill, heading north-west across the Celles road and then turning west once they were in thick forest. The next day all but two swam the fast-flowing river Meurthe. On the western bank they split up and Lieutenant Jim Silly led three men through the woods towards the village of Menarmont. Here they encountered a German patrol and in the firefight that followed Silly and Private Donald Lewis were separated from the other two.

What happened next is, to an extent, based on conjecture and vague accounts given by French and German eye-witnesses.

The memorial stone at Le Harcholet. The building in the background stands on the site where Lewis, Brown and a French fighter were brutally killed.

Donald Lewis was only 18 when he met his death. His father strove to discover the truth behind his death and corresponded regularly with Eric Barkworth.

In his interim report on the missing men, Major Barkworth wrote that Silly, Lewis and Private Selwyn Brown may have been taken together to Schirmeck, an assumption made on the evidence of two German guards at the camp. This wasn't in fact the case.

Lewis and Brown were executed together (at Le Harcholet) but mystery remains as to how they were caught. In his account of their exfiltration, Corporal Larley listed the ten men in MacGibbon-Lewis's party but made no mention of Selwyn Brown. Was this an oversight? The 36-year-old Brown was a veteran of 2SAS; in December 1943 he had participated in Operation 'Sleepy Lad' in eastern Italy, a five-man mission to sabotage the east coast railway and harass road transport. Brown had parachuted into the Vosges on the night of 21/22 September as part of MacGibbon-Lewis's stick, and he later acted as his officer's front gunner when they embarked on jeep patrols. It seems likely therefore that he was among MacGibbon-Lewis's party when they set off from the sawmill on 9 October for the American lines.

It is probable that Brown and Lewis were caught together. Brown, whose parent regiment was the 9th Queen's Royal Lancers, was twice the age of the 18-year-old Lewis and he may have taken the unseasoned teenager under his wing.

The last hours of their lives were spent in the company of a third man, a young Maquisard. According to local legend, this man was the illegitimate offspring of a wealthy industrialist who lived in the region, a result of a brief liaison with a young working-class woman, possibly one of his domestic staff. The man paid the woman to keep their secret and after the son's death, he used his influence within the town hall to remove all records of the birth, as he didn't wish to tarnish his name. As the Maquisard had used a *nom de guerre*, the identity of this brave young man, so grotesquely rejected by his father, has never been established.

There were two witnesses to the murder of Lewis, Brown and the Frenchman. The first, Victor Launay, described in a statement in December 1944 that on the afternoon of 16 October a British prisoner was brought to his isolated house in the hamlet of Le Harcholet, 1½ miles south-east of Moussey. The prisoner remained in the kitchen with two Germans while three other soldiers searched the premises. Once done, the Germans called out to another house and their comrades appeared with two other prisoners. The Frenchman said in his statement that one of the British prisoners was wearing glasses, which led to the mistaken assumption that this man was Lieutenant Silly. The witness may have been mistaken, or it may have been the Maquisard wearing glasses.

Another eyewitness in Le Harcholet was Madame Fernard Benoit, who watched as 'two prisoners in khaki and a civilian in dark clothes' were led from the house of Victor Laumay into a shed adjoining a house known as the Maison Quiren Joseph. She made no mention of any prisoner wearing glasses. Four German soldiers appeared in the house of Madame Benoit demanding straw. She watched the Nazis take the straw into the shed. 'A few seconds later the shed began to burn,' she stated. 'I then heard two long bursts of machine-gun fire followed by three pistol shots. Three Germans then returned to my father's house for more straw, which they obtained. As they left, they were laughing.'

Madame Benoit had one other remark to make: 'I believe the victims were hung up before the burning as I could see human forms through the flames.'

A few metres from the shed where Lewis, Donald and the unknown Frenchmen were murdered is a memorial stone (**GPS 48.424010, 7.044599**) on which is a plaque explaining in French the fate of the trio. The plaque states that the men were shot outside the shed and their corpses then thrown inside the burning shed, which contradicts the version given by Madame Benoit only a few weeks after the brutal killing.

To reach the memorial stone from Moussey, drive south on the D49 towards Le Saulcy, but in the middle of Le Harcholet, where the road forks (**GPS 48.422282, 7.038279**), take the left fork, marked 'champs Genêts' for a few hundred metres until you reach another fork (**GPS 48.422218, 7.045183**). Head left on the lane called Pré Matré, and the rebuilt house and memorial stone are on the right after 200 metres.

The murder of Jim Silly

It has never been determined how and when Jim Silly was captured, only that following his apprehension the young officer was held in the cellar of the school in the town of Étival-Clairefontaine. It was here he gave his address to Maurice Simon, one of several Frenchmen held in the makeshift cell. The young Milicien Yvette Demetz also identified Silly as the Englishman to whom she served food while he was a prisoner. The school still exists, although its official title is now the Ecole Du Vivier. It is located on 2–10 Place de la Résistance, Étival-Clairefontaine (**GPS 48.360836, 6.862987**).

On 22 October Silly and thirteen Frenchmen were removed from the school and driven approximately 5 miles north into what is known locally as the Vallée de Ravines. On reaching the Barodet sawmill, the prisoners were herded inside and massacred by machine-gun fire. The sawmill was then burned to the ground and it was another six weeks before investigators sifted through the charnel house, discovering among other items the steel frame of Silly's spectacles.

There is an annual ceremony on 22 October at the monument erected close to the site of the execution (**GPS 48.411614, 6.919173**) and the stone foundations of the sawmill are still visible among the undergrowth. It is a gloomy, eerie spot, deep in the forest, redolent of wrongdoing.

To reach the site from the pretty town of Moyenmoutier, head north on the road marked Route de la Haute Pierre in the direction of St Prayel. On reaching St Prayel, turn right at the crossroads in the middle of the hamlet on the road called Route des Sagards and continue on this road for just under 2 miles. The monument is on your right and the ruins of the sawmill on the left of the road.

The remains of the fourteen men were removed from the sawmill and buried in a mass grave in the cemetery of Moyenmoutier (**GPS 48.375796, 6.912487**). This lies on the hillside on the south side of the town, close to the imposing abbey. There is a car park by the cemetery. Enter by the gate in the bottom corner and take the path up the middle towards the top of the

Jim Silly lies in Moyenmoutier cemetery along with the Frenchmen massacred with him in the Vallée de Ravines.

cemetery. Silly is the only British soldier in the cemetery and his distinctive CWGC headstone can be found 5 metres to the right of the path, about two-thirds of the way up the cemetery. When I visited there was a perspex tablet placed by the Silly family, commemorating Jim's parents and sister Frances, who died in 2012 aged 91. Behind Silly's headstone is one that honours the thirteen Frenchman who were murdered in the sawmill.

The only other Allied serviceman in the cemetery is an American from the First World War, Thomas Rodman Plummer. His grave is against the back wall at the top left. He was a first lieutenant in the American Red Cross and, although too old to see active service, he volunteered for the Red Cross in 1917 and ran the Franco-American Mobile Canteen No. 31 at Moyenmoutier, where American 'doughboys' did their training prior to going into the trenches. He died aged 56 on 24 November 1918, presumably of Spanish influenza.

The murder of James Black's Party

Lieutenant James Black was only 19 when he parachuted into the Vosges on the night of 6/7 September as part of Major Reynolds' reinforcement stick. Also inserted that evening was 30-year-old Corporal Harry Winder and his pal, Private James Salter, like him a Lancastrian, as well as Privates Len Lloyd, a former sapper from London, and James Dowling.

Four days later, early on the morning of 11 September, the SAS base was compromised by an enemy patrol that Brian Franks estimated to be thirty strong. Surprise was on the side of the SAS so Franks 'sent Lieut. Black and his stick to cut them off and ambush them down the path but unfortunately Lieut. Black was not sufficiently quick in obeying my order to catch them in time'.

Franks withdrew east across the Plaine valley to a pre-arranged rendezvous at the Lac de la Maix, north of Moussey, but Black and his men were never seen again. One SAS soldier told Franks that he 'thought that he heard Bren gun fire half an hour after leaving'.

It is known that Black and his men reached a house at the hamlet of Les Colins, 3 miles east of the SAS camp. They brewed some tea at the invitation of the owner, Madame Yorg, and left in the early evening in the direction of a sawmill known as La Turbine. Here they encountered three more SAS soldiers: Sergeant Frank Terry-Hall, Corporal Thomas Ivison and Private Jack Crosier. Also present was a Frenchman called Gaston Mathieu. He played the part of a friend, offering to guide the eight soldiers to their rendezvous at the Lac de la Maix. Instead he turned them over to the Nazis. There was a shoot-out at the sawmill in which Black was wounded in the leg. The French couple who lived next to the sawmill – Léon Marchal and Maria Thirion – were summarily executed by the Nazis. There is a small roadside memorial to the pair (**GPS 48.479044, 6.985458**) by the site of the sawmill, which today is a private house, although the foundations of the sawmill are visible in the back garden.

The SAS prisoners were taken to Raon l'Etape, where they were held for one night. Next morning they set out on foot but Black's painful leg wound held them up and so the Germans commandeered a milk truck to a house in Badonviller. From there they eventually found their way to Schirmeck, where Black's wound was dressed.

They weren't long at the camp, although at their trials the Gestapo officers Wilhelm Schneider and Erich Isselhorst gave differing accounts as to the exact sequence of events. Ultimately, the eight men were driven to some woods south of the town of Saint-Dié-des-Vosges and executed. A memorial stone, unveiled in 2019, marks the approximate spot (**GPS 48.279182, 6.901446**).

After the war the dead men were disinterred and, curiously, reburied in the country of the men who had taken their lives. Their graves are in the CWGC cemetery at Durnbach, 30 miles south of Munich (**GPS 47.778252, 11.733635**).

The murder of Lieutenant David Dill's party

When Lieutenant Colonel Brian Franks decided to wrap up Operation Loyton, he detailed six men to wait for an overdue sabotage party to return in order to guide them through the lines; the half dozen were selected by Franks for their reliability: they were Lieutenant David Dill, Sergeant Ralph 'Jock' Hay, Lance Corporals George Robinson and Fred Austin, and Privates Jimmy Bennett and Edwin Weaver, who preferred to be called 'Ted'.

A day later there was no sign of the overdue sabotage party but instead Dill and his men were found by a detachment of Germans, who had been tipped off as to their whereabouts by a French informant, reportedly a woman called Jacqueline Weber. There was a fierce firefight for an hour before Dill, realising their position was hopeless, surrendered. According to a young Maquisard who had remained with the British, the German officer congratulated Dill on his stern resistance, shaking him by the hand and declaring: 'You are my prisoner; you are a soldier and so am I.'

Dill and the five men were taken first to the factory of Monsieur Gerard, where they were treated as normal POWs. The next day the Gestapo collected the soldiers and drove them to the small town of Saâles, to their HQ, Maison Barthlemy, in the rue de l'Eglise. Here they were reunited with four of their comrades, Captain Victor Gough, the leader of the Jedburgh team that had arrived with Henry Druce's advance party on 13 August, and three SAS soldiers: Peter McGovern, Reg Church and Walter Nevill.

On the morning of Sunday, 15 October the eight British soldiers were ordered from their cells, leaving Dill and Gough inside. They were led handcuffed into a lorry driven by Georg Zahringer. 'I was ordered to drive along the road leading from Saâles to Grand Fosse,' he stated at his war crimes trial. He was told to pull over when they reached 'a spot where there was a thick fir

The house where Lieutenant Dill and the rest of the SAS rearguard were taken after their capture and held prior to their execution.

'We were good men': the last words of Edwin Weaver, and now immortalized on the memorial to him and his comrades.

wood on both sides of the road'. The tailgate of the truck was lowered and the first prisoner was ordered out. This was Reg Church, a 24-year-old Londoner. He was ordered to strip, and then he was frogmarched into the woods. A few seconds after he disappeared from sight there was a gunshot. 'The remaining English prisoners on the truck did not say anything, but remained silent,' commented Zahringer.

One by one the eight soldiers were led to their deaths, shot in the back of the head as they stood on the lip of a freshly dug pit. The last to die was Ted Weaver. When he climbed down from the truck Weaver stood facing his executioners: 'We were good men,' he told them.

Ralph Hay's grave at Durnbach in Germany as it was in 1947.

There is a memorial at the site of the men's execution (**GPS 48.339355, 7.031799**), which was unveiled in 2019 in the presence of many of their relatives. It is an impressive and original design, the dedicated work of a post-war SAS veteran, and close by is an information board describing the events and listing the men, alongside a photograph of each one. It is at the fork of the D32 and the C23, approximately 5 miles west of Saâles. The Gestapo HQ where the men were held, the Maison Barthlemy in the rue de l'Eglise, is now a retirement home. Some 9 miles north of Saâles, on the D49, is the factory of Monsieur Gerard at Le Harcholet (**GPS 48.418623, 7.044986**), where Dill and his five comrades were first held after their capture. When I visited in 2016 the house was in a state of decay, a once-elegant white three-storey building crying out for some attention.

The eight men shot at Grand Fosse were also reinterred after the war at Durnbach war cemetery, 30 miles south of Munich.

Gaggenau

Lieutenant David Dill and Captain Victor Gough were told that their comrades were being transported to a POW camp. They may have suspected otherwise. Gough had sent a message to SAS Brigade HQ on 15 September stating that Sergeant Seymour had been captured on 17 August and 'shot as reprisal'. But Seymour had not been shot because he cooperated with the Germans.

Gough and Dill did not talk, and they paid for their silence. A young Maquisard imprisoned with them in Saâles, Roger Souchal, recalled that in the days after the eight soldiers had been taken away, 'Dill, Gough and I were beaten'. Dill came in for particular attention. The Germans wanted to know the location of 'the colonel' (Brian Franks). 'He came back crying,' said Souchal of Dill after one particularly violent interrogation. 'But he had not told them.'

On 20 October Dill and Gough – who had been captured some time in late September – were taken to Schirmeck. Over the coming days they were joined by more of their comrades, including Majors Denis Reynolds and Anthony Whatley-Smith. They had been caught together as they attempted to exfiltrate at the end of October. Curiously, on 18 September a small party of French SAS, operating independently of Loyton, but just a few miles north of their British comrades, had a brief skirmish with some Germans. The Nazis fled, and among the items retrieved by the French was 'an SAS jumping jacket with D.B. Reynolds written on the collar'. Reynolds' middle name was Bingham. It was unwise of Reynolds to have written his name in his jacket and unwiser still to have lost it. Possibly he removed the jacket on the DZ as he adjusted his clothing after his parachute jump, and forgot all about it.

Reynolds and Whatley-Smith, who was known as Andy, were taken individually for questioning at the Nazi HQ in Maison Barthlemy, Saâles.

Interrogations took place in the cellar where the screams could not be heard. Reynolds was flayed so severely, recalled Abbé Hett, a prisoner at Schirmeck, that his ribs were visible.

By mid-November the Americans were only a few miles from Schirmeck, and on the 17th of the month its commandant, Karl Buck, was instructed by BDS chief Erich Isselhorst, to shoot 'all inmates of the cells and such special persons as I might select'. He was also told to release the female prisoners and then burn the camp.

Buck disobeyed the order because he 'did not consider it wise to leave fresh mass graves behind'. Instead, on 21 November he drove 75 miles north-east to Gaggenau in Germany, a town just outside Baden-Baden, and 'arranged with the Mercedes-Benz factory for a supply of sufficient trucks to evacuate the male prisoners from Schirmeck across the Rhine'.

The evacuation began that same evening and continued until the night of 22/23 November when the last truck left Schirmeck. Inside were ten Allied prisoners: Dill, Gough, Reynolds, Whatley-Smith, and Privates Maurice Griffin and Christopher Ashe, the latter a member of Operation Pistol, who had become separated from his unit on inserting into the region in the middle of September. Griffin had parachuted into Loyton with Franks' party but a few days later he was described by his CO as being unable to participate in offensive patrols as he was 'medically unfit'. Four days later he was captured although it is not known how. Also inside the truck were four American airmen who had been captured after baling out. A few hours after the truck's departure, on the morning of 23 November, the Americans liberated Schirmeck.

The ten prisoners weren't in Gaggenau for long. They and four members of the French clergy left in a truck in the early afternoon of 25 November in the direction of the Erlich forest. One of the guards, Heinrich Neuschwanger, described what happened next: 'We turned right along the track for a distance of about 75 metres and then stopped. [Erwin] Ostertag asked me how many prisoners we should do at a time. I suggested three, so he gave the order for the first three to jump down. The first three were civilians. I remember that as we were marching them down the track one of them took a photograph out of his pocket and looked at it. We turned into the wood for a distance of 20 to 30 metres until we came to the bomb crater (the pre-arranged execution site). On a signal from Ostertag, who was walking in the middle, we each fired at the prisoner in front of us.'

The three Nazis stripped the dead to make them unrecognisable, and they stole whatever took their fancy, including a gold pocket watch and a small leather document case. Then they returned along the track to fetch three more prisoners. It took half an hour to kill them all, and by the end the Germans had lost the appetite for rummaging through the pockets of their victims.

left to right:
(I) Dürrmann. (II) Constanzer, (III) Lipps. (IV) Nussberger. (V) Ostertag.
(VII) Armbruster.

German guards. Ostertag is third from the right.

A ceremony at Moussey in August 1945 to mark the return of inmates from Naztweiler, attended by 2SAS representatives (note the flag).

The endgame of an evil ideology. The dead of Gaggenau.

Dill's army issue wristwatch remained on his left arm and a chunk of chocolate still in its English wrapper was in a pocket of his trousers.

On 13 May 1945 the bodies were removed from the bomb crater and re-interred first in Gaggenau's municipal cemetery and then in the war cemetery in Durnbach. It is believed that a further thirteen prisoners were also executed in Erlich forest in November 1944, and a memorial stone was erected in their honour in August 1947 close to where they met their deaths (**GPS 48.799826, 8.333147**).

There is also a memorial plaque in the former camp site, the 'Mahnmal Sicherungslager Rotenfels', inaugurated in the spa gardens in 1985. In 2018 the plaque was incorporated into a remembrance site which includes a section of the foundation walls of two of Gaggenau's prison barracks (**GPS 48.809409, 8.301063**).

Moussey

No other place has such a strong emotional bond with Operation Loyton than Moussey, known locally after the war as the 'town of widows'. The inhabitants paid a fearful price for their loyalty to the Maquis and the SAS, with 140 of the 220 men deported by the Nazis never returning home. One who did survive deportation and spells in Auschwitz and Dachau was Henri Poirson. When I met Henri in the summer of 2016 he told me that the scars of what

Moussey suffered during the Occupation took many years to heal. Inhabitants, particularly the wives and mothers of the men who died in captivity, resented the fact that Henri had returned, and frequently he was abused in the street. Gradually, the pain subsided, replaced by a quiet pride in the town's collective courage and stoicism. This was nurtured by the survivors of Operation Loyton, who never forgot the fidelity and the fortitude of the French. In his operational report, written shortly after he had returned to England, Lieutenant Colonel Brian Franks remarked: 'All the villagers of Moussey were first class. In Celles and the Celles valley, the people were terrified, and of little help. In Moussey, where we were welcomed, we were obviously looked upon as the spearhead of the Liberating Forces. The fact that we have now left the area and brought much misery and unhappiness to the villagers, is a point which should not be overlooked, and I feel they will consider themselves let down by us.'

Franks and Christopher Sykes were among a small contingent of 2SAS who returned to Moussey on 18 August 1945 to attend a service of commemoration for the dead. They had been invited to form the guard of honour. The SAS, wrote Sykes, decided to make use of the visit to 'form a military cemetery for those of our men who had been killed in battle or been murdered by the Germans in the valleys of the Vosges highlands'. He continued: 'It was characteristic of the generosity of this sorely oppressed place that they should have asked us to bury our dead among their own. I repeat again that had it

The church at Moussey. Henri Poirson told the author that the belfry was used by the Maquis as an observation post.

Henri Poirson, a Maquisard who was sent to Auschwitz, was one of the few men of Moussey who returned home. Pictured here in 2016, he died a few months later.

not been that they helped us as they did, or had we not been there to be so helped, most of their tragedies would have been avoided.' Sykes recalled that melancholy shrouded Moussey. Women in mourning clothes shuffled along the streets as the church bells pealed almost daily for another requiem mass for a man who had been confirmed dead. In time, a memorial was erected on the corner of Rue René Laederich (**GPS 48.430791, 7.024983**) on which were listed the names of those who died as a result of deportation.

In 1979, three years before his death, Brian Franks attended an armistice day service at Moussey in the company of several other veterans from Loyton,

Looking south-west from Moussey church at the Rocher du Mont, behind which lay the DZ on which the SAS landed on 13 August.

The SAS flag in Moussey church, a symbol of the strong bond that still exists.

including John Hislop and Peter Power. Also in attendance was a detachment from 21 SAS, the territorial regiment, who parachuted into the region to the delight of the locals. The British veterans, along with their Maquis counterparts, attended a service in Moussey church and later there was a lunch at which Franks gave a brief speech: 'The loyalty of the French never wavered and without this loyalty we would never have succeeded in defeating the enemy,' he told his audience.

In the south-west section of the churchyard of Moussey (**GPS 48.425383, 7.016145**) are the headstones of ten of the soldiers from Operation Loyton who lost their lives. Nearly all were murdered by the Nazis. One of the gravestones is that of Sergeant Robert Lodge, who was killed during the firefight on 17 August (not the 18th, as indicated on his headstone). Lodge's real name was Rudolf Friedlaender and he was a German Jew. He chose 'Lodge' as his nom de guerre because it was the surname of his fiancée, Win. He fought off the Germans with his Bren gun for long enough for most of his comrades to withdraw. He also wanted to kill as many Nazis as he could. It was never his intention to surrender to his countrymen. The British army pathologist who examined Lodge's body stated in his report that the bullet removed from his skull was from a British revolver, which 'certainly lends some support to the statement of some Germans that he committed suicide'. Lodge was awarded a posthumous DCM, the citation praising his 'complete disregard for his

It was thanks to the endeavours of the SAS war crimes team that the dead were traced, identified and laid to rest with dignity in Moussey.

The graves of Selwyn Brown and Donald Lewis in Moussey.

personal safety, a fine offensive spirit and a gift for leadership much above the average'. The inscription on Lodge's headstone was chosen by his father, Max, and was a quotation from a letter his son had written to him not long before his death. It reads: 'Our sacrifice will not be futile if the survivors have learned the lessons of this disastrous war.'

Selwyn Brown and Donald Lewis, who were murdered in such despicable fashion at Le Harcholet, were laid to rest side by side in Moussey, along with the young Frenchman who died with them, still unknown. Also in Moussey churchyard is Gerald Davis, the Phantom signaller who was betrayed to the Nazis by the priest of Le Saulcy church. Davis was taken to Schirmeck where he was interrogated by Wilhelm Schneider. The Nazi tried without success to beat out of the Englishman the location of the SAS camp. Then Davis was given an ultimatum: if he refused to cooperate, he would be shot. He was given ten minutes to think it over. One can only imagine what went through Davis's mind in those ten long minutes. It would have been so easy to answer their questions. He wouldn't have to say much, just point out some locations on a map. But Davis rejected the easy option. The inscription on his headstone reads: 'Loyal unto Death.'

Chapter Five

Jacob to Judas

For many months Sergeant Kenneth Seymour was believed dead, 'shot as reprisal', as the telegram from Victor Gough to Special Forces HQ stated on 15 September 1944. On 21 February 1945 the fate of the wireless operator was decided in an internal SOE memo that declared he was 'not believed to be prisoner of war but has in fact been notified as killed in action'. The War Office Casualties Branch was notified, Seymour's pay book was cancelled and his death was officially recorded.

A little over a fortnight later word came through via the Red Cross that Seymour was not in fact dead; he was a prisoner of war. On 12 March that year Lieutenant Colonel D.L.G. Carleton-Smith, at Special Forces HQ, wrote to Seymour's parents at their home in Surrey. 'It is difficult to know what to say to you, and these are anxious days I know, but I trust that you will have him home again before very long,' he said. 'I know his friends in the unit will be delighted that he is safe.'

Seymour was repatriated in early April 1945 and spent a short time at the Connaught Military Hospital in Surrey. On the 10th of that month he wrote to Carleton-Smith about two matters; the first was to ask if his fellow members of Team Jacob, Captain Victor Gough and Captain Maurice Boissarie, were still alive. The second question was about money, and in particular Seymour wished to know 'why no special pay has reached my account?'.

Carleton-Smith replied that Boissarie was dead (killed in a shootout with the Nazis on 4 September the previous year at Viombois) and that Gough had last been heard of in November as a POW. He asked Seymour for a detailed report of his capture, interrogation and incarceration, which he received in May. It ran to six pages and described how Seymour had valiantly fought the Germans before being captured. He was then subjected to 'various interrogation' but Seymour stated he had 'expressed complete ignorance' and revealed nothing about the wireless. On the basis of what he read, Carleton-Smith recommended Seymour for a Mention in Despatches, which was gazetted on 30 August 1945.

Seymour became a local hero, praised in the *Sutton Times and Cheam Mail* for his courage and fortitude in surviving Gestapo interrogation and several months of captivity.

Ken Seymour was the only prisoner from Operation Loyton who returned home.

But gradually Seymour's heroism began to unravel, thanks to the unstinting efforts of Major Eric Barkworth and his 2SAS War Crimes Investigation team. There had from the outset been a curiosity as to why Seymour alone of the thirty-one men captured during Operation Loyton had survived. As Barkworth began interrogating some of the Gestapo responsible for the torture and execution of the SAS men, it became apparent why Seymour had not ended up in an unmarked grave in a forest.

The German detainees were eager to talk, desperate to curry favour with their captors in the hope of escaping the gallows. On 20 November 1945 Marie Uhring recounted a conversation with his superior, Wilhelm Schneider, not long after the capture of Seymour. 'Schneider told me the wireless operator had "talked"',' stated Uhring. 'I do know Schneider told me that the captured wireless operator had shown how to work the wireless set and the cipher.'

Two days later Barkworth questioned another Nazi, Julius Gehrum, who said: 'I was also present during the interrogation of the first prisoner with the injured foot [Seymour]. I noticed that the prisoner with the injured foot answered Schneider's questions, and Schneider said to me afterwards, with this man we can begin something.'

Schneider was himself a prisoner and on June 1946 he stood trial charged with multiple counts of murder. Major Hunt, the chief prosecutor for 21 Army Group, asked him about the wireless operator.

> 'You interrogated Seymour, did you not?'
> 'Yes.'
> 'And you thought you could get something out of Seymour, did you not?'
> 'Yes.'
> 'And you have said that you did get something out of Seymour, have you not?'
> 'Yes.'
> 'And unless you were lying, you got some very important information out of Seymour, did you not?'
> 'It was very important at the time.'
> 'And it was military information, was it not?'
> 'Yes.'
> 'Seymour was not shot, was he?'
> 'No.'

Wilhelm Schneider incriminated Seymour at his trial. He was hanged for his crimes in 1947.

Major Hunt then asked Schneider about two other SAS prisoners he had interrogated, Private Wally 'Ginger' Hall and Sergeant Gerald Davis. The Nazi confirmed that neither prisoner had revealed anything under interrogation other than their name, rank and number. Both were taken away and shot.

Three days later Seymour appeared as a witness for the defence. Why he did so is a mystery. It was at Schneider's request, but the court did not have the power to force a repatriated British soldier to take the stand. He could have refused. Did he feel indebted to Schneider because he had not been shot along with his comrades? Or, more likely, was he forced to attend by the

SAS, who by now were aware that Seymour was not the hero he had claimed to be, although he continued to deny the Germans' accusations of collaboration. Nevertheless, in an initial report about Loyton's war crimes written before the trial, Barkworth had concluded that Seymour 'was not reluctant to give information'.

Major Hunt asked Seymour if he had any idea why he was the only captured SAS soldier not to have been executed.

'None at all,' replied Seymour. 'My only thought about it is that I was first to be captured.'

'I am a little puzzled,' said Hunt. 'You gave false information, you say, to the Germans?'

That was correct, responded Seymour. He had given false information about the lights used by the SAS on drop zones for approaching RAF aircraft on resupply runs.

'Did nobody come to you and tell you they had tried the information?' asked Hunt.

'No, nobody at all,' replied Seymour.

Hunt asked Seymour why he had told this to the Germans. Shouldn't he have just given his name, rank and number?

'I do not really know,' he said

Hunt then put it to Seymour that he had not been threatened by Schneider during his interrogation, implying what Barkworth had written in his report, that the wireless operator had not been 'reluctant' to talk to his interrogator.

'Well, it is difficult to remember these little things,' said Seymour. 'It is nearly two years. At that time I did not worry about what anybody looked like or took any notice what people were saying.'

Schneider was found guilty of murder and hanged in January 1947, while other members of the Nazi police unit responsible for the torture and execution of SAS soldiers were handed sentences ranging from four to ten years. The British press was dismayed at what it viewed as a derisory punishment. 'It is difficult to understand the comparatively small sentences,' reported the *Observer*. 'A lenient attitude to such abomination is surely as unwise as the ill-treatment of ordinary prisoners is unworthy.'

No further action was to be taken against Kenneth Seymour. Back on Civvy Street, Seymour attempted to put the past behind him. He married (and fathered four children) and enrolled in teacher training college in the late 1940s. That was his profession for the rest of his working life, first as a technical drawing teacher and later as a teacher of mathematics in a Hertfordshire school. According to Colin Burbidge, the nephew of Captain Victor Gough, in 1979 Seymour contributed an article to his school magazine about his wartime exploits. 'Several claims he made in this article for the school magazine were patently wrong,' wrote Burbidge. 'A footnote to this article declared it was the only time he wrote about or disclosed any details of his wartime activities.'

Among the inaccuracies made by Seymour were the date of Operation Loyton (he stated it had begun on 7 June 1944) and his declaration that no trace of his dead comrades was ever found: this despite the fact he had attended the war crimes trial when the court heard gruesome details of the discovery of their bodies.

When I interviewed Henry Druce in 2003, the leader of Loyton's advance party acknowledged that none of the SAS had undergone resistance to interrogation training prior to the operation. Furthermore, he said that the 'Germans could be very persuasive if ever they caught you'. However, added Druce, as far as Seymour was concerned, 'I have always been led to believe his betrayal was freely given'. In short, he concluded, Seymour was 'a traitor'.

Druce's remarks appeared in my book, *Stirling's Men*, which was published in September 2004. The following month Kenneth Seymour died aged 83.

Chapter Six

Legends of 2SAS

Harry Vickers

Born in 1921, the son of a veteran of the First World War, Harry Vickers enlisted in the Cheshire Yeomanry territorials prior to the outbreak of war in 1939. He subsequently joined the Royal Engineers and during the Blitz spent a few months in a bomb disposal team before being posted to Gibraltar working on building airfields. In search of some more excitement, Vickers volunteered for 2SAS in November 1943 while the regiment was on operations in Italy.

A neat diligent man, with a dry sense of humour and a phlegmatic nature, Vickers was posted to C Squadron in 1944 under the command of Major Roy Farran. As a leader, recalled Vickers, Farran 'was out on his own but I must also mention [Captain] Jim Mackie. He was a magnificent man; nothing frightened Jim and he didn't mind being at point when we drove through France, that's where he wanted to be.'

Vickers was equally unflappable and gained a reputation early on in Operation Wallace as a resourceful and steady NCO. His first contact with the enemy was on 23 August as C Squadron drove towards their operating base in the forest of Châtillon, and Vickers inflicted several casualties on the Germans with a Bren. He was surprised at how calm he remained, even when enemy bullets were snapping off leaves from the bush under which he was positioned. 'You didn't think too much or else you'd frighten yourself,' he reflected. 'Does that sound daft? It was one thing at a time.'

Vickers was awarded a Distinguished Conduct Medal for his part in Operation Wallace, in particular his courage during the battle of Châtillon. Vickers spent the winter of 1944/45 with his squadron at Balavil House in Scotland (the location for the BBC drama *Monarch of the Glen*). It was there that Colonel Brian Franks informed his men of Hitler's Commando Order, which had led to the murder of dozens of SAS officers and men in the preceding eighteen months. 'Franks got us all together and told us that a lot of our lads had been tortured,' remembered Vickers. 'We were given the opportunity to leave the regiment, no ill-feelings or recriminations. We were all perfectly free to leave. Nobody left.'

Vickers crossed the Rhine on 25 March and his squadron was attached to the 6th Independent Guards Armoured Brigade, tasked with spearheading

Harry Vickers (*third from the right*) at an Operation Wallace reunion in Chatillon in 1982. Also in the photo are Roy Farran (*fifth from the right*) and Tanky Challenor (*second from the right*).

the advance towards Munster. On 29 March he was on a three jeep patrol under the command of Lieutenant Lord John Manners. 'The side roads were nothing more than muddy lanes and one jeep got bogged down within sight of some Germans a couple of fields away,' he said. Vickers and the two men in his jeep were ordered to attack the enemy from their flank while the rest of the patrol launched a frontal assault. During the attack Vickers suffered a serious gunshot wound to his arm, bringing his war to an end. 'The bullet had shattered the bone and taken about a two-inch chunk out of my arm and I was in hospital for a year.'

In December 1946 Vickers received his DCM at Buckingham Palace, the citation praising 'his grim determination to inflict casualties on the enemy. His jeep alone accounted for some twenty enemy vehicles and his ceaseless courage was an inspiration to his whole troop.'

Vickers was an estate surveyor in the old Ministry of Works for many years and was a regular at regimental reunions, a popular and modest man among his fellow veterans. 'I made a bit of a splash for myself in France,' he reflected in 2002, 'but I didn't do a lot really.' He died in 2007.

Ralph Hay

Ralph Hay was one of those sergeants that every officer dreams of having under his command. Reliable, durable and equable, the Scot volunteered for 2SAS in the autumn of 1943. He had joined the army eight years earlier, aged 16, and his first posting overseas was to Malta in 1938.

Ralph Hay, photographed at the start of the war, was a brave and resolute soldier.

His first officer in the SAS was Lieutenant Quentin Hughes, nicknamed 'Jimmy'. The pair knew each other from the Royal Artillery and had served together in a battery of 18-pounders in Malta during the height of the Axis air attacks in the winter of 1941/42. Hughes remembered Hay as 'a charming Scots boy, easy going, placid and entirely dependable under any circumstances. He was just the sort of rock that was needed to balance my volatile character.'

In late 1943 Hay was by Hughes's side throughout training, enduring long route marches and acquiring the skills of guerrilla warfare, including sabotaging railway lines. In January 1944 Hughes was selected as the second-in-command of a small team that embarked on Operation Pomegranate, the objective of which was to parachute into Occupied Italy and destroy aircraft at San Egidio. Hay, on the other hand, returned to Britain with 2SAS in the spring of 1944 and underwent further training in Scotland. In August that year he was selected by Captain Henry Druce as one of the advance party in Operation Loyton. Druce summarised Hay as 'a very fine man'.

Hay's qualities came to the fore during the tense weeks of Operation Loyton, and he was one of the few soldiers that Druce came to trust implicitly. The CO of 2SAS, Colonel Brian Franks, shared Druce's view about Hay. When Loyton began the hazardous task of withdrawing through the German lines on 6 October, Franks chose Hay as one of the six men to remain behind to wait for an overdue SAS sabotage party to return to their forest hideout. The six were betrayed by a French informant to the SS, who took them prisoner after a fierce firefight. A little over a week later Hay and his comrades were driven into the dark forest of the Vosges and executed.

For many months Hay's parents in Scotland had no news of their son. Then, on 6 July 1945, an article appeared in the newspaper headlined 'Paratroops Tortured and Shot' in which it was claimed that several 2SAS soldiers had suffered such a fate after being captured in the Vosges. Major Roy Farran wrote to the Hays and told them to ignore the reports, stating that 'there is no reason to believe that Sgt Hay met his end in an unpleasant way'.

The Hays doubted the veracity of Farran's well-intentioned letter and contacted the War Office. By now a 2SAS investigation, headed by Major Eric Barkworth, was under way, and on 16 August 1945 the War Office wrote to Mr and Mrs Hay, saying: 'I am directed to state, with deep regret, that although your son was one of a party captured by the enemy in October 1944, from close investigation made on the Continent it must be concluded that he died after capture ... it is presumed that they were shot after capture and that death occurred on or shortly after the 16th October.'

Druce recommended Hay for a Military Medal but to his chagrin the Scot was awarded only a posthumous Mentioned in Despatches. 'There is no such thing as justice in this world,' reflected Druce in 2003.

Anthony Greville-Bell

Few SAS soldiers have enjoyed such a varied and colourful life as Anthony Greville-Bell. Having joined the SAS in late 1942, he served with the regiment for two years, taking part in a sabotage mission in Occupied Italy, Operation Speedwell, for which he was awarded a Distinguished Service Order. The citation described his 'outstanding powers of leadership and unfailing judgement in most difficult circumstances'.

Tony Greville-Bell (*right*) in 2002 at the grave of Thomas Bintley, killed on Operation Trueform. In the middle is George Daniels, Greville-Bell's sergeant in 2SAS.

He was seconded to the French SAS for a brief period in the spring of 1944 as a liaison officer and in August that year he commanded Operation Dunhill, when they parachuted into Normandy. On returning to England he was attached to the Political Intelligence Department of the Foreign Office.

Greville-Bell rejoined the SAS when it reformed as 21SAS, a territorial regiment, and expected to be sent to Korea in 1950 but instead his squadron was posted to Malaya to fight Communist insurgents, where they were incorporated into Mike Calvert's Malayan Scouts (redesignated 22SAS in 1952). Greville-Bell and Calvert didn't see eye to eye. The former believed that Calvert did not understand the SAS creed and in Malaya Greville-Bell was 'horrified to find he had built a fort in the middle of the jungle'. This was a tactic Calvert had pioneered with the Chindits in Burma in 1944.

Greville-Bell left the army in 1956 and for a while worked in the city, an experience he found tedious. In 1958 he made headline news in the UK when he sued his second wife for divorce on the grounds that she had committed adultery with the Duke of Primo de Rivera, the Spanish Ambassador to the Court of St James's.

Greville-Bell's face was again splashed across the front pages in September 1963 when he was arrested in Spain and sentenced to four years' imprisonment. His crime was to have smuggled tobacco into the country in 1949, a charge he denied. The arrest caused a diplomatic incident and Greville-Bell was released after two weeks.

He subsequently moved to LA where he wrote soap operas and had three scripts turned into films, most memorably the 1973 cult Hammer film, *Theatre of Blood*, starring Diana Rigg and Vincent Price.' But I absolutely hated Hollywood,' he reflected. 'It was the absolute opposite of everything in the SAS – crooked, mean and insincere.' On returning to Britain he worked as a commercial sculptor, married twice more, and launched an amateur opera company in his Chelsea neighbourhood.

Beneath the suave, sophisticated and insouciant exterior was a sharp, unorthodox and innovative mind that found its niche in irregular warfare. But perhaps Greville-Bell's greatest asset was his cheerful stoicism. 'The whole defence against the horrors of war was to make a joke of it,' he told the author in 2002 when discussing SAS operations that went awry. 'You don't seethe against anyone, it's funny, you just laugh about it and say what a bloody balls-up. One gets so used to it in the British army, or any army. The thing about war is that you plan and plan but the ones that win are the ones who are most able to overcome disasters because nothing ever goes the way it's supposed to.'

François Martin

Born in 1916, François Martin was a talented artist who was accepted into the prestigious Beaux Arts school in Paris in the 1930s. Had it not been for the

François Martin (*middle*).

war, he might have achieved fame as a painter; instead he found his calling as a guerrilla soldier. He enlisted in France's famous *Chasseurs Alpins* and saw action in the Norwegian campaign in April and May 1940.

Following the fall of France, Martin evacuated to England where he joined the Free French. Promoted to Aspirant, an officer designate rank, he shipped out to the Middle East in October 1940 and after several months of inactivity he volunteered for L Detachment, SAS, in May 1941. He was involved in the jeep operations behind enemy lines in July 1942, under the command of Augustin Jordan and Andre Zirnheld. One of his fellow SAS officers, Carol Mather, recalled the joie de vivre that emanated from the cave hideout of the French contingent: 'There would be much singing and much laughter and talk of Cairo and girls and cinemas.'

Martin, who kept warm at night under his long hooded *Chasseurs* cloak, drove one of the three French jeeps that participated in the Sidi Haneish raid on the night of 26/27 July 1942 when the SAS destroyed eighteen German aircraft and damaged a further twelve. The following morning the French patrol was attacked by three German Stukas and Zirnheld was mortally wounded. Martin buried his friend in the desert with a cross made out of a packing case and scratched with a bayonet the inscription 'Died for France'.

Martin assumed command of Zirnheld's section and took part in the Benghazi raid of September 1942 before joining David Stirling's B Squadron following the enlargement of L Detachment into the 1SAS Regiment. B Squadron began operating in western Libya in late November 1942, harassing the Axis forces as they withdrew west from El Alamein.

Casualties were heavy, owing to the inexperience of many officers and men, and by January 1943 only Jordan, Martin and Stirling remained of B Squadron's initial intake of officers. The three rendezvoused on 21 January and plotted to attack the enemy between Sfax and Gabes. Only Martin evaded falling into enemy hands. His patrol mined some roads and railway lines before their presence was betrayed by some Arabs to the Germans. Forced to abandon their jeeps, Martin led his men across the desert on foot for three days before encountering an American unit. 'They described us in an American magazine as wild, bearded and burnt brown, like five Robinson Crusoes,' remembered one of the Frenchmen, Alain Papazow.

On his return to Britain in the spring of 1943, Martin was personally presented with the Croix de la Libération by General de Gaulle and he was promoted lieutenant in 4SAS, one of the two French regiments, under the command of Colonel Bourgoin. His death on 12 July 1944 robbed the SAS Brigade of one of their most experienced, respected and admired officers. He was, reflected Carol Mather, 'a most charming, brave and excellent person'.

Roy Farran

There is a tale, perhaps apocryphal, that Roy Farran once complained to Paddy Mayne, the legendary commanding officer of 1SAS, that the Irishman didn't think much of 2SAS. To which Mayne replied: 'Not at all, Roy ... I don't think anything of 2SAS.' If it was true, then it was said with Mayne's customary dry humour, nothing more than a barb born out of friendly rivalry. The Irishman was a magnanimous man and also one who had a natural instinct for guerrilla fighting. He was an admirer of Bill Stirling, who raised 2SAS in 1943, and in Farran he recognised a soldier not dissimilar to himself.

Farran came to irregular warfare late in the war, in the summer of 1943, after distinguishing himself in action with the King's Own Hussars. 'In a transit camp outside Algiers I met an old friend called Sandy Scratchley,' he recalled after the war. 'He was a well known steeplechase jockey and he said "Well Roy, why the hell don't you join 2SAS?"' In Bill Stirling, Farran had a superlative mentor, a deep strategic thinker and a fiercely independent-minded officer. 'Bill was more of a planner than a leader on the ground, but all the same he was a very, very great soldier and he played a great part in Britain's eventual victory in the war.'

Farran learned that, far from their gung-ho image, and their rather pejorative nicknames such as 'private armies' and 'cafe gangsters', the SAS's chief function in the war was not killing enemy soldiers. 'It was occupying ground and if the enemy feel so nervous that they retreat, you've won the battle and with minimum casualties,' explained Farran. 'The SAS opened up a new flank, in a way; they made the enemy very nervous about his rear areas.'

After seeing action in Italy in 1943, Farran led Operation Wallace in August and September 1944, the most effective of all 2SAS missions in Occupied France. 'It was a good operation, I was quite proud of it,' he said. 'Our instructions were to create hell across France ... I'm only sorry that the SAS histories don't reflect the big success it was.'

Farran returned to Italy in 1945, leading Operation Tombola, the objective of which was to harass withdrawing German troops, and when the war ended he had been rewarded with the DSO, three MCs, the Croix de Guerre and the American Legion of Merit.

The end of the war was not a smooth transition for Farran. His counterinsurgency skills were deployed by the British in a police unit tasked with quelling the Jewish resistance in post-war Palestine. His methods were brutal and he was accused of murdering a 16-year-old boy, although he was never charged. Jewish terrorists sent him a letter bomb, addressed to 'R Farran', but it was opened by his younger brother Rex, resulting in his death.

Roy emigrated to Canada in the 1950s, where he put his flair for writing (his book *The Winged Dagger* is one of the best SAS memoirs) to good use as a journalist and, later, as the editor of the *North Hill News*, the country's leading weekly newspaper.

He returned on several occasions to France to participate in remembrance events, including a ceremony in 1994 where he received the Légion d'honneur from the French government. Farran's last visit was in 2001, when he laid a wreath on the memorial to Bill Holland in Châtillon. He died five years later aged 85.

Lessons learnt for SAS units
By Captain Pierre LeBlond
(Operation Dingson)

A. First of all an <u>iron discipline</u> must be enforced. Most of our troubles come from the undisciplined or imprudent going to seek food without orders, taking meals at farmhouses and so on. I have the names of two paratroops (who paid for their lack of discipline with their lives) who were in part responsible for the breaking up of SAMWEST base.

B. Discipline alone is not enough. Paratroops must be first-class infantry and know every single dodge and trick of the trade. Unfortunately, they are nothing of the sort. This becomes particularly clear at night. I made a night march of over 120 kms with seven of my men, whom I had constantly to remind of these essentials:

i) March on the verge and not on the road itself.
ii) When I was in the lead and stopped to listen, no one else stopped at the same moment, so that for eight or ten seconds I couldn't hear a thing.
iii) Silence and discretion.
iv) Avoid talking loud by night and talking too much by day.

C. Avoid overloading rucksacks. 65 lbs should be regarded as the outside limit.

D. Don't carry too much food; it can be found on the spot. Take coffee and sugar, which are warmly welcomed and useful for barter.

E. Take care over storage of rucksacks. Never prime grenades and explosives in them – indeed do not carry detonators in the same rucksack as explosives. Each party commander must check that this has been complied with before emplaning, and in particular that no one is carrying primed grenades in his pockets.

F. Don't be afraid of giving yourself trouble – never hesitate to march that extra mile to avoid a village on which you have no information. It is better to get dirty on a muddy path than to take the main road. It is better to sleep hard than to be wakened in bed at four in the morning by the Gestapo. It is better to march by night and sleep by day. It is better to avoid using cars and bicycles (on the main roads).

G. When you cannot avoid asking civilians for help, ask for it in a big way; nine out of ten will welcome you warmly, but:
  i) Only ask help of the peasants. Avoid refugees like the plague.
  ii) Avoid built-up areas and only make the isolated farms.
  iii) Avoid letting yourself be seen, let alone spoken to, by children, who always talk. These peasants never trust even their own children for this sort of work.

H. Pay well for what you use.

I. Never talk politics except to talk it down. When with the partisans try to make them see that it is mainly political differences that prevent unity and so delay their liberation.

J. Do not hesitate to change into plain clothes to carry out a task if it offers advantages. If you are captured you are shot however you are dressed. As a rule, intelligence and liaison tasks are the only ones for which plain clothes would be needed. In any case when in plain clothes one must carry a really well forged identity card. Take identity photos taken in plain clothes into the field. For getting cards forged only apply to someone really reliable.

K. Do not believe every tale you hear. Here is one example – a small motor-car arriving in a village with three Boche had been magnified by the end of two hours to two lorries and thirty Russian cavalry. Always take precautionary steps if the news is alarming, but take care to verify and check your information before you act.

L. Beware of cider – it is stronger than you think – and still more of Calvados, also called La Goutte and Le Fort. It will often be put before you, but you must remember how much you need to keep your head clear.

Personal kit carried by SAS Phantom Patrol

Per Man

1   .45 Automatic and holster
1   ''   spare mags and pouches
1   Dubbin
1   Life belt Mk2
1   Knife fighting
1   ''   single blade folding
1   Trousers, paratroops
2   Vests, string (too heavy for hot weather)
1   Flashlights US 122A with 1 spare Bty (excellent)
1   Rucksack, Bergen, rubber lined
1   Bedding roll, Icelandic with cover (cover too heavy)
1   Entrenching tool with cover
1   Map case, 'P' type
1   Oil bottle, gause and rod
20 rds Amn .45 spare
1   Mess tin
1   Waterbottle
1   Ground sheet
4   Prs socks, spare
1   Shirt, spare
1   Pullover, worn
1   Gym shoes prs
1   Washing kit
3   Pencils
3   Message pads, small
1   First field dressing
1   First aid pack (add foot powder)
1   Steel helmet with net (never used after jumping)
1   Smock, Airborne, camouflaged
1   Jumping jacket (never used after jumping)

1   pr Short puttees (gaiters would be better)
4   Boxes matches
1   Escape pack
2   Secret compasses
1   Escape money purse (£12)
1   Language booklet
3   24hr ration packs
2   Face veil camouflaged
4   Handkerchiefs
1   Compass, oil
1   pr Binoculars
1   Watch GS
1   Housewife
1   Luminous ball (not really of use)
1   Anti-dog smell (never used)
1   Map sets of the area
1   Gas cape (optional), most useful for bivouacs
1   Knife, fork, spoon, mug set
1   Carbine American with 5 mags .300
1   Haversack American type

Carried in the Patrol

2   Jedburgh sets complete with 6 crystals
2   MCR1 with 2 bts each
2   Protractors
2   Code books and 3 silks
2   India rubbers
4   Sets rubber heels and soles
5   Escape maps (2 paper, 1 silk) sets
5   Grenades no. 36
2   Sets of colour filters for torches

Appendix III

Citation for Henry Carey Druce, DSO, 5 November 1944

Capt. Druce was in command of a reconnaissance party of ten all ranks which was dropped by parachute into the Eastern Vosges on 12 August 1944. Unfortunately the arrival of this party was known to the enemy who sent a force of approximately 3,000 men from Strasbourg to round them up. For the next two weeks the detachment was continually harried and though often without food and in an exhausted condition, were able through Capt. Druce's brilliant leadership not only to evade the enemy but also to inflict casualties upon them which were out of all proportion to the size of his force.

Later, when reinforcements arrived and Capt. Druce handed over command to a senior officer, there was no task, however dangerous, that this officer was not prepared to undertake. On many occasions at great personal risk Capt. Druce entered enemy occupied towns and villages in order to obtain information which was vital to future plans.

On one occasion he drove in a single jeep in daylight through the town of La Petite-Raon and Moussey, both some 50 miles behind the enemy lines and strongly garrisoned with troops. In both cases he caused great confusion and considerable casualties to the enemy. The degree of confusion can be judged by the fact that approximately 250 enemy troops withdrew in disorder from Moussey in the belief that a superior Allied forced had arrived.

Finally, on 29 September, Capt. Druce was ordered to contact 3 US Army carrying important documents and much useful information of enemy dispositions. Not only did he succeed in this mission but on receipt of information from 3 US Army which he considered vital to his commanding officer, he decided to attempt to pass through the enemy lines once more with this information. This was accomplished successfully. In all, Capt. Druce passed through the enemy lines on no less than three occasions.

This officer's skill, energy, daring and complete disregard for his own safety won the admiration of not only all British troops with whom he came in contact, but also that of the local French people amongst whom his name became a byword.

Report on SAS Operations

Strength Deployed

1SAS Regiment	425
2SAS Regiment	425
3 French Parachute Battalion	500
4 French Parachute Battalion	485
Belgian Independent Company	130
HQ SAS Troops Signal Section	22
Total	1,987

In addition, a certain number of 2SAS Regiment, 3 French Parachute Battalion and Belgian Independent Company have been landed twice or more in different areas. 200

GRAND TOTAL 2,187

Casualties

Figures are only very approximate as certain personnel from 2SAS Regiment may still be safe but behind the enemy lines, and other figures have not been confirmed.

	Lost in aircraft	Killed	POW	Missing	Total
1SAS	14	18	30	12	74
2SAS	8	16	14	40	78
3 French	3	60	–	–	63
4 French	–	59	–	48	107
Belgian Coy	–	5	–	–	5
SAS Signals	–	–	–	3	3
Total	25 (1%)	158 (8%)	44 (2%)	103 (5%)	330 (16%)

Results Achieved

This falls under many different headings and figures quoted must necessarily be pure estimates, worked out on a conservative basis. In some areas small parties worked with FFI and figures are not available to be included.

a) Enemy casualties, excluding prisoners, inflicted by SAS troops alone or when directly assisted by FFI under command – 3,500–4,000.

b) Enemy prisoners. SAS troops, together with FFI and Allied armies, assisted in forcing 15/20,000 enemy to surrender near Bourges, and many hundred prisoners were taken in other areas in Brittany, Vendee, Vienne and the Rhone Valley.

c) Enemy transport seriously damaged or destroyed – 750–1,000 vehicles.

d) Enemy trains destroyed – 25

e) Enemy rail communications. It is impossible to summarize briefly as many lines were kept permanently closed by FFI or SAS, but apart from these over 50 effective cuts were carried out.

Glossary

AU –Auxiliary Units were highly trained guerrilla fighters whose job, in the event of a German invasion of Britain, was to wage irregular war against the Nazis.

BCRA –Central Bureau of Intelligence and Action, the Free French equivalent of SOE, who were one component of the Jedburgh teams.

BDS –Befehlshaber der Sicherheitpolizei, the Nazi security police.

Bren gun –Czech-made light machine gun with a range of 2,000 yards.

DCM –Distinguished Conduct Medal.

DZ –Drop zone for paratroopers and supplies.

Einsatzkommando –Nazi mobile killing squads that operated in eastern Europe and later in France.

Eureka/Rebecca – A short-range radio navigation system that was used for the dropping of airborne forces and their supplies. The system consisted of two parts: the Eureka was a ground-operated transponder, which emitted a single morse letter to the Rebecca transceiver inside the approaching aircraft, enabling the pilot to home in on the DZ.

FFI – Free French Forces of the Interior, the formal name for the resistance fighters.

Gestapo – Geheime Staatspolizei: the secret police force of Nazi Germany.

GHQ – General Headquarters.

Hauptsturmführer – A Nazi Party rank with equivalent seniority to a captain.

IDS – Inspekteur der Sicherheitspolizei: a senior rank within the BDS whose role was to oversee all Security Police and SD units in a specified region.

Jedburghs – Special operations paratroopers who operated in Occupied Europe to coordinate airdrops, train local resistance fighters and liaise with SHAEF HQ in the UK. They were composed of Americans, British and Frenchmen.

Jeep – The American Willys jeep that was first used by the SAS in July 1942 in the North African campaign.

L Detachment – The initial name given to the special force founded by David Stirling that later became the Special Air Service regiment.

Maquis – The disparate armed Resistance groups formed in France from 1942 onwards. The word 'Maquis' refers to a type of Mediterranean vegetation.

MC – Military Cross.

MCR1 – Miniature Communication Radio Receiver, developed for the Special Operations Executive.

Milice – The French fascist paramilitary organisation established by the Vichy regime in 1943 to work with the Nazis against the Maquis.

MM – Military Medal.

NCO – Non-commissioned officer.

OSS – Office of Strategic Services, the American equivalent of SOE, who were one component of the Jedburgh teams.

Phantom – Also known as GHQ Liaison Regiment, this was a reconnaissance unit first formed in 1939.

PIAT – Projector, Infantry, Anti Tank, a hand-held weapon that fired a 1kg bomb and was effective up to a range of approximately 100 metres.

POW – Prisoner of War.

RAF – Royal Air Force.

RHSA – Reich Security Headquarters.

RSM – Regimental Sergeant Major.

RTU – Returned to Unit, the fate of special forces soldiers who fail the selection course.

SAS – Special Air Service, formed in 1941.

SHAEF – Supreme Headquarters Allied Expeditionary Force.

SBS – Special Boat Squadron, formed from D Squadron 1SAS in March 1943.

SD – Sicherheitsdienst, the intelligence service of the SS.

SFHQ – Special Forces HQ, at Baker Street. London, which oversaw all clandestine operations including SOE and SAS.

SOE – Special Operations Executive, formed in 1940 to conduct espionage and sabotage in Occupied territory.

SRS – Special Raiding Squadron, formed in 1943 from 1SAS and which reverted to that regiment at the end of the year.

SS – Schutzstaffel: the paramilitary force of Nazi Germany.

Standartenführer – A Nazi party rank in which the officer commanded a Standarte, equivalent to an army battalion of up to 500 soldiers.

STO – Service du travail obligatoire: a forced labour scheme introduced in France by the Nazis in 1942 that resulted in the deportation of hundreds of thousands of French workers to Germany to work for their war effort.

Vickers K – Rapid firing machine gun designed for aircraft and later used by the SAS.

W/T – Wireless telegraphy.

Further Reading

Note: Book titles in **bold** are in French.

Barbu, Philippe, *Operation Wallace* (Association des Amis du Chatillonnais, 2017).

Burbidge, Colin, *Preserving the Flame* (self-published, 2008).

Farran, Roy, *Winged Dagger* (Collins, 1948).

Flammand, Colonel Roger, *Paras de la France Libre* (Presses De La Cité, 1978).

Ford, Roger, *Fire from the Forest* (Cassell, 2003).

de Galzain, Michel, *Le Bal du Ciel* (Galles, 1964).

Harrison, D.I., *These Men Are Dangerous* (Cassell, 1957).

Hislop, John, *Anything But a Soldier* (Michael Joseph, 1965).

Kemp, Anthony, *The SAS at War 1941–45* (Penguin, 1991).

Kemp, Anthony, *The Secret Hunters* (Michael O'Mara, 1986).

Mackay, Francis, *SAS Trooper: Charlie Radford's Operations in Enemy-Occupied France and Italy* (Pen & Sword, 2011).

Mortimer, Gavin, *Stirling's Men: inside story of the SAS in WW2* (London, Weidenfeld, 2004).

Mortimer, Gavin, *The SAS in World War II: An Illustrated History* (Osprey, 2011).

Mortimer, Gavin, *The SAS in Occupied France, 1SAS Operations* (Pen & Sword, 2021).

Mortimer, Gavin, *David Stirling: The Phoney Major* (Constable, 2022).

Otway, Lt Col. T.B. *The Official History of Airborne Forces* (HM Government, 1946).

Ricatte, Rene, *Viombois: Haut Lieu de la Résistance* (2nd edition, Muller, 2005).

Strawson, John, *A History of the SAS Regiment* (Book Club, 1985).

Sykes, Christopher, *Four Studies in Loyalty* (Collins, 1946).

Index